DATE DUE

OCT 1 - 1996	

Maurice R. O'Connell

DANIEL O'CONNELL: THE MAN AND HIS POLITICS

Daniel O'Connell

THE MAN AND HIS POLITICS

Maurice R. O'Connell
Emeritus Professor of History, Fordham University

WITH A FOREWORD BY
Conor Cruise O'Brien

IRISH ACADEMIC PRESS

The typesetting for this book was produced by
Gilbert Gough Typesetting, Dublin, for
Irish Academic Press Ltd,
Kill Lane, Blackrock, Co. Dublin.

BRITISH LIBRARY CATALOGUING IN PUBLICATION DATA
O'Connell, Maurice R. (Maurice Rickard)
Daniel O'Connell: the man and his politics
1. Ireland. Politics. O'Connell, Daniel 1775-1847
I. Title
941.5081'092'4

ISBN 0-7165-2446-5

Printed by
Betaprint Ltd, Dublin

Contents

Foreword

Having read these essays, I found that I had a much clearer view of O'Connell, both as man and as politician, than I had before, although I had read the best-known biographies. Maurice O'Connell, the editor of Daniel O'Connell's *Correspondence*, knows more about Daniel O'Connell than any other living person does. The essence of that learning is lucidly distilled in this book of essays, and made readily accessible to the general reader.

Maurice O'Connell writes about his great ancestor with respect, but not leaving out the warts. There are not many of these, and those that there are — chronic extravagance is about the worst — are no more than the excess of some good quality — the good quality in this case being generosity.

I found my respect for O'Connell, which was already considerable, deepened and enlarged by these essays. In that sense, the essay which made the most impact on me was 'Ireland, Irish Americans and Negro slavery'. The contrast between O'Connell's position and that of the Young Irelanders, in relation to slavery, is indeed striking and may upset the preconceptions of many readers.

In the Republican tradition with which I was familiar in my youth — though I subsequently managed to shake it off pretty well — the Young Irelanders were ardent idealists filled with burning zeal for liberty. O'Connell, on the other hand, was a clerical reactionary, or opportunist. If that was so, you would expect, would you not, that the Young Irelanders would have been passionately opposed to slavery, while O'Connell would have advised caution, and practised circumlocution?

Yet, as Maurice O'Connell shows, the reality was precisely the reverse. Daniel O'Connell would accept no money, for his Repeal fund, from the United States if it came from a slave State, or from any source connected with slavery. The Young Irelanders repeatedly rebuked him for this excess of zeal. In the Repeal Association in March 1845, O'Connell declared: 'I want no American aid if it comes across the Atlantic stained with Negro blood.' Thomas Davis, who was present, respectfully recorded his dissent:

> I don't think it would be quite just towards myself, and towards those
> who concur with me, if I did not to some extent express my dissent
> from the opinion put forward by my illustrious friend in reference to
> the American slaveholders. I condemn slavery as much as it is
> possible to condemn it . . . but I am not prepared to condemn the
> Americans to the extent to which my illustrious friend goes, or
> silently to hear the amount of censure which he so conscientiously
> and so consistently with his opinions casts upon them.

Even apart from the substance, the style of Davis's dissent on this occasion
is unattractive. But O'Connell had the effect on the Young Irelanders of
making them go on in this mealy-mouthed vein. Maurice O'Connell
speaks of the Young Irelanders' 'ambivalent praise' of Daniel O'Connell.
This is something of an understatement, in reference to some of the
statements quoted in the essay, 'O'Connell, Young Ireland and Violence'.
Some of these reek of malice, combining with fulsome reverence in a most
unappetizing manner. Take the following, from a speech by the Young
Irelander Doheny:

> But I trust our great leader shall not the less estimate, or the less truly
> appreciate, the feelings of gratitude and respect which I entertain for
> him, because in the same bosom I entertain a feeling of respect for
> myself, and I cherish the highest respect for the expression of truth
> everywhere.

There is no political leader anywhere who could listen to that language
without murmuring to himself: 'Watch out for the knife!'
    Of course, we can understand the predicament of the Young Irelanders.
To express a difference of opinion with Daniel O'Connell at a meeting of
the Repeal Association in the 1840s was a delicate enterprise. O'Connell
had no qualms about encouraging what later came to be called a 'cult of
personality'. That cult was part of his political stock-in-trade throughout
the Emancipation and Repeal agitations. And O'Connell's followers were
quick to resent any departures from that cult. So that the feigned obeisances
and the coded language were part of the protective colouration of a
dissenting minority. They are a kind of negative tribute to the compelling
power of the personality of Daniel O'Connell in his day.

Daniel O'Connell was both a strong Catholic and a strong liberal. It was
an unusual combination in his day, and it is still somewhat unusual. I doubt
whether many of the millions of Irish Catholics who followed Daniel
O'Connell in the agitation for Catholic Emancipation would have felt

much enthusiasm for Jewish Emancipation. Yet O'Connell, having achieved — or completed — Catholic Emancipation, went on to help and advise those Jews who were working for Jews to be admitted to the Parliament of the United Kingdom. Together with his passionate detestation of Negro slavery, O'Connell's advocacy of Jewish Emancipation, is among the proofs of the solidity of his commitment to human liberty, and not merely Irish liberty. In that respect, as in others, O'Connell towers over the Young Irelanders.

The essay that is of greatest relevance to our life in this island today is that on 'Religious Freedom'. Maurice O'Connell quotes a number of interesting statements by Daniel O'Connell on this subject. Two of these seem to be so relevant to us as to warrant quoting them in this Foreword. They run:

> I entirely agree with you on the principle of freedom of conscience, and no man can admit that sacred principle without extending it equally to the Jew as to the Christian. To my mind it is an eternal and universal truth that we are responsible to God alone for our religious belief and that human laws are impious when they attempt to control the exercise of those acts of individual or general devotion which such belief requires.

And

> My firm belief is that the duty of every man is to be a Catholic whilst I abhor every attempt either by direct penalty or by any civil exclusion to bring the law in any way in aid of my creed. I am indeed unequivocally a voluntary.

These are statements which we, in modern Ireland, should think about. On the face of it the spirit of those statements seems to run counter to the inclusion in our Constitution of laws designed to implement certain prohibitions of specifically Catholic provenance: the laws against abortion and divorce. I am not, please, about to tell you, what Daniel O'Connell would have to say, 'if he were alive today'. All we can say for sure about Daniel O'Connell, 'if he were alive today', is that he would be 214 years old.

No, I am thinking about Daniel O'Connell, *as he was in his own day.* Among Catholics of the mid-nineteenth century, Daniel O'Connell was a resolutely advanced liberal, and internationally recognized as such. We of the late twentieth century have shown ourselves, in two referenda, to be ready 'to bring the law in aid of our creed', something which O'Connell said he 'abhors'.

Those of us who have been significantly affected by the Republican tradition are accustomed to think of O'Connell as 'too clerical'. But we ourselves, in this Republic of ours, have shown ourselves to be, in practice, more clerical than O'Connell was in his day. We have a lot to learn still, from O'Connell.

I therefore hope that this fine book, from which so much can be learned, will be widely read in Ireland. In conclusion, I wish to congratulate Irish Academic Press for its initiative in publishing *Daniel O'Connell: The Man and his Politics.*

CONOR CRUISE O'BRIEN

Preface

Two years ago Michael Adams of Irish Academic Press suggested that I gather the ten articles I had written on Daniel O'Connell for publication as a book.[1] On my retirement from Fordham last year I found he was still of this opinion so I prepared the material for this new venture.

The articles included here originally appeared in journals or essay collections, the first being pubished in 1970. I have decided to arrange them chronologically as they appeared, with the exception of the short biographical essay, published in 1987, which I now present as the last article.

Because of overlapping, some passages in the original articles have been omitted, and two of the articles — on Negro slavery — have been amalgamated into one. I have made no changes in interpretation. On two points my interpretation has changed since writing the earlier articles. I no longer see O'Connell as totally opposed to the Colleges Bill of 1845 and I no longer see the Young Irelanders as totally in favour of it. Two historians, Professor Oliver MacDonagh of the Australian National University at Canberra and Professor Kevin B. Nowlan of University College, Dublin have independently come to the conclusion that O'Connell's aim in the great Repeal campaign of the 1840s was very probably major reform and not Repeal. I now accept that interpretation.

1   Chapter One originally appeared as 'Daniel O'Connell: income, expenditure and despair' in *Irish Historical Studies*, XVII, No. 66 (September 1970), pp. 200-220; Chapter Two as 'Daniel O'Connell and Religious Freedom' in *Thought*, Vol. 50, No. 197 (June 1975), pp 176-18; Chapter Three as 'Daniel O'Connell and the Irish Eighteenth Century' in *Studies in Eighteenth-Century Culture*, Vol. 5, edited by Ronald C. Rosbottom (Wisconsin University Press, 1976), pp. 475-495; Chapter Four as 'O'Connell Reconsidered', in *Studies*, LXIV, No. 254 (July 1975), pp. 107-119; Chapter Five as 'O'Connell, Young Ireland and Violence', in *Thought*, Vol. 52, No. 207 (December 1977), pp 384; Chapter Six as 'O'Connell and his Family', in Donal McCartney, ed., *The World of Daniel O'Connell* (Mercier Press, Dublin, 1980), pp. 19-28; Chapter Seven as 'Daniel O'Connell: Lawyer and Landlord' in Kevin B. Nowlan and Maurice R. O'Connell, eds., *Daniel O'Connell: Portrait of a*

He would certainly have loved to gain Repeal, but he must have known that the British Government would never concede it, at least not until long after his day.

Dr Conor Cruise O'Brien, the most distinguished Man of Letters in Ireland today, has kindly agreed to write the Foreword to this book.

I should like to thank the editors of the various publications in which these articles appeared for their courtesy and interest, and, where necessary, for granting permission for re-publication.

MAURICE R. O'CONNELL

Dublin, March 1989

Radical (Appletree Press, Belfast, 1984; Fordham University Press, 1985), pp. 107-120; Chapter Seven as 'Irish Constitutionalism: a Rescue Operation', in *Studies*, Vol. 75, No. 299 (Autumn 1986), pp. 318-327. Chapter Nine is an amalgam of two articles: 'Daniel O'Connell, Romantic Nationalism and Negro Slavery', which will appear in *Thought* in 1989, prior to publication here, and 'Daniel O'Connell, Irish Americans and Negro Slavery', which appeared in *The Record*, the journal of the American Irish Historical Society, New York (Winter 1988), Vol. 3, No. 1, pp. 61-68. The last chapter was published as the Daniel O'Connell entry in *Great Lives from History, British and Commonwealth Series* (Salem Press of California, 1987), pp. 1988-1993.

1

Income and expenditure

The barony of Iveragh in Co. Kerry forms the extreme western part of the peninsula that runs out from Killarney. It is mountainous and weather-beaten tourist country, facing the Atlantic and separated from the rest of Ireland by a range of mountains. The O'Connells had been the principal family in the barony for some centuries before Daniel O'Connell was born in 1775. Several branches of his family along with other Gaelic families — McCarthys, O'Mahonys, O'Sullivans and Sugrues — had survived the turmoil and confiscations of the sixteenth and seventeenth centuries and the penal laws of the eighteenth. By the time of O'Connell's birth these families were small landlords — frequently middlemen — whose distinction owed more to lineage and 'following' than to landed wealth. The one substantial landlord among them was Maurice O'Connell of Derrynane, usually known as Hunting-Cap, the head of the senior branch of the O'Connells. As a smuggler, farmer and landlord, by lending money to landlords and by thrift he had greatly increased his inherited property so that by the beginning of the nineteenth century he could be described as a rich man. A childless widower, he adopted his nephew Daniel as his heir.

Daniel's father, Morgan O'Connell, had imitated Hunting-Cap's economic example but on a smaller scale. He lived at Carhen, a mile to the east of the present small town of Cahirciveen which was then only a hamlet, ran a general store, reared ten children of whom Daniel was the eldest son, and died prosperous in 1809. Like Hunting-Cap he had added to his inherited property and bequeathed the bulk of it to Daniel. The future political leader was thus the heir to two estates, one of them substantial.

As a young barrister who showed promise, O'Connell was the hope of his family, a family which owing to its religious background had good reason to know the value of prudence, application and thrift. Then in 1802 he upset all calculations by marrying for love his distant cousin, Mary, one of the eleven penniless children of Thomas O'Connell, a Tralee physician who had died while most of his children were still young. Knowing how

Hunting-Cap would regard an impecunious marriage he kept it secret for six months until he could visit Derrynane and put his case persuasively before 'the old gentleman', as he usually called him. The reaction was even worse than he had feared: they quarrelled and he was disinherited.[1]

A year later Hunting-Cap made a will in favour of O'Connell's brother John, having arranged for him to marry Miss Elizabeth Coppinger, a Co. Cork heiress. Mary reported to her husband that 'your mother told me in confidence last night that . . . the old gentleman would settle the entire of his landed property on John but would not tie himself down to settle more than ten thousand pound on him'.[2] Later she wrote:

> Your father had a letter this day from your Uncle O'Mullane mentioning your uncle [Hunting-Cap], the king (as he calls him), had told him he had made a will in John's favour since his arrival in Cork in consequence of your having run counter to his wishes. Thank God, he can't do more. . . . The old sinner, he will never have such a representative as the one he has so shamefully given up.[3]

O'Connell's parents accepted his marriage but his father caused concern three years later by altering his will in order to leave his youngest son James part of his property. Mary begged her husband not to be angry:

> Consider that you have every prospect of making a fortune independent of the dirty trifle taken from you and left to James, and consider also, heart, that you have a wife who doats of you and who would be equally as fond of you were you in poverty as in affluence.[4]

In 1806, however, his father settled the bulk of his landed property on O'Connell entailing it to his eldest son, which meant that O'Connell would only have a life interest and could not sell the property.[5]

For three years after their quarrel Hunting-Cap remained on formal terms with his nephew, employing him as a legal adviser on his business dealings. Then in March 1806 a reconciliation took place at the Cork assizes, and O'Connell informed his wife

> As to the meeting with my uncle, nothing could be pleasanter to me. He told me of the hereditary property being mine and gave me most distinctly to understand that he intended all the rest for me. He told Robin Hickson that he had forgiven me.[6]

In 1809 Hunting-Cap gave him £750 to purchase land in Iveragh, and in the following year he appears to have given him nearly £2,000 for additional purchases and, some months later, a further donation in land.[7] In 1811 O'Connell's gross rental amounted to £2,400.[8] The bulk of this was obviously the property of his father, who had died in 1809. Out of it he had to pay head rents, a jointure to his mother of £227 and a mortgage interest of £224.[9] In 1819 O'Connell's uncle, Lt-Gen. Daniel Charles, Count O'Connell, now in retirement from the pre-revolutionary French army and living in France, estimated that his nephew's income from land had fallen from over £2,000 to perhaps £1,500.[10] The reduction was probably due to the long depression that followed the end of the Napoleonic wars. In 1823 his brother, James, estimated O'Connell's income from land as 'a clear £1,000 a year'.[11] This reduced figure could mean that O'Connell had sold some of the land that he owed to Hunting-Cap's bounty, but, then, James was a pessimist and enjoyed underrating income. In 1813 Hunting-Cap settled a large property on O'Connell, entailing it on his eldest son and that son's male heir but keeping the income for the duration of his own life.[12] This estate settled in 1813, and that settled on him by his father in 1806, both being entailed, were passed on by O'Connell at his death to his eldest son Maurice.[13] In 1848 they were estimated as having a net rental of some £2,600.[14]

O'Connell's income at the bar rose steadily from £255 in 1801 to nearly £4,000 in 1813.[15] The depression following the Napoleonic wars seems to have affected a reduction in earnings since he makes several references to the sparsity of legal business on the Munster circuit (the one on which he always went) from 1814 until early 1817.[16] In later years his fee book shows the following earnings: 1822 - £5,057; 1823 - £5,157; 1824 - £6,045; 1825 - £3,893; 1826 - £4,497; 1827 - £4,868; 1828 - £5,178.[17] The sharp drop in 1825 was due to the fact that he spent nearly three months in England in the early part of that year when an emancipation bill was passed by the commons but rejected by the lords.

Even as a young man O'Connell had broken with his family's tradition of thrift. When he was a law student his mother received the following complaint from Hunting-Cap:

> He is, I am told, employed in visiting the seats of hares at Keelrelig, the earths of foxes at Tarmons, the caves of otters at Bolus and the celebration of Miss Burke's wedding at Direen — useful avocations, laudable pursuits for a nominal student of the law. The many indications he has given of a liberal mind in the expenditure of money have left a vacuum in my purse as well as an impression on my mind not easily eradicated.[18]

When about to be called to the bar he was cautioned by his uncle against renting expensive accommodation in Dublin

> One maxim you should always keep in view which is that it is, by
> much, more decent and reputable to advance gradually and as cir-
> cumstances will prudently admit in expense than to set out ostenta-
> tiously and soon be obliged to recede and retrench.[19]

Even if not already in debt O'Connell said goodbye to solvency when
he purchased No. 1 Westland Row in Dublin, into which his family moved
in July 1805. Money was short, and he wrote to a friend:

> The purchase of my house and the first expense of getting into it have
> made it extremely desirable to me to get the use of £200 for a year
> but it is still much more necessary for me that no third person should
> know that I wanted or got the money. . . . This is the first serious
> favour I have ever asked of any person.[20]

Lending money was another foible. In 1806 he told his wife that his
kinsman, Mountain Mahony, had just paid him £100 'which I never
expected to get',[21] and drew from her the illuminating comment: 'how
fortunate you were in getting the money from Mahony. I wish all those
who owe you money would *surprise* you as he has done'.[22] Two years
later, in asking her husband to send her money from Limerick, where he
was on circuit, Mary wrote:

> Should you, my darling, not send me up the money as you earn it,
> you will be tempted to *distribute* it when you go to Kerry. It is there
> all the claims are on you, putting Splinter[23] first of all.[24]

His extravagance became more marked in 1809 when he moved from
Westland Row to the fashionable Merrion Square, to No. 30, on the south
side, now No. 58. Mary was frantic:

> For God's sake, darling love, let me entreat of you to give up this
> house in the Square if it is in your power, as I see no other way for
> you to get out of difficulties. If you borrow this money [one thousand
> guineas] for Ruxton, how will you pay it back? In short, love, I
> scarcely know what I write I am so unhappy about this business[25]

Going security for friends and relatives was another and more dangerous
weakness. In 1811 when Hunting-Cap heard that a Kerry connection, John
Primrose, might ask O'Connell to secure him for a large sum he warned,

> I can scarcely express to you the uneasiness I feel since this matter

has occurred to me, well knowing, as I before mentioned, the softness and facility of your disposition and with what ease designing men may draw you into their measures when in fact and in truth acceding to such a proposal from Primrose must have the effect of inevitably ruining you beyond redemption. I therefore again and again most earnestly caution you against it and further add that no feeble or temporising excuses will have any sort of weight with me and that your neglecting to comply with what I not only so earnestly beseech and request but what I absolutely and decidedly command, will create a breach between us never to be healed.[26]

By 1815 his wife seems to have extracted from him a promise not to lend money or go security or, at least, not to do so without telling her.[27] In March of that year Mary was informed by her husband's brother, James, that he was involved as security in the bankruptcy of James O'Leary, a merchant in Killarney. The blow was all the greater now because the country was in the grip of economic depression. Mary wrote her husband a furious letter. It is not extant — he did not keep his wife's letters when they were hurtful — but his reply can be quoted in full:

My darling, darling Mary,

I can write but a few words to you today. Indeed I cannot write more. I never in my life was so exquisitely miserable as your last letter made me. I wept over it for two hours this morning in bed and I am ready to weep over it again. When once suspicion enters the human mind there is an end of all comfort and security. It is, I see, in vain to make any protestations to you. You are, I see, irrevocably unhappy. I blame, indeed I do, my brother James for instilling this poison into your mind. I know he did it for the best but it was a cruel experiment to render the sweetest, the dearest, the tenderest, the best, the most beloved of wives and mothers unhappy on a loose and idle suspicion. Indeed, indeed, indeed, you have no cause for uneasiness but my heart is too full and I cannot write more.

Tell my Nell [his eldest daughter], my angel Nell, that I will write to her as soon as I can.

Darling, believe me, do believe me, you have no cause for your misery. Did I ever deceive you?

Ever, sweetest Mary,

Your most tenderly and faithfully doating
Daniel O'Connell.[28]

But Mary was forgiving: 'I know it is not in your nature to deceive me.

Let me then, darling, entreat of you to forget what is past and do not for one moment think me capable of having no confidence in your pro-testations'.[29]

In telling Mary that she need have no cause for uneasiness O'Connell was either unduly optimistic or was merely trying to still her fears, for O'Leary's financial crash was a very serious matter. It appears to have involved O'Connell in an enormous debt, as suggested by a letter which Mary wrote to her husband more than a year later:

> Dumas [an attorney in Killarney] told me that there was not a greater buck in Bond Street [London] than Mr James O'Leary, dashing away at his usual rate and most elegantly dressed at the opera and theatres every night and living at one of the most expensive taverns in London. This is the way, darling, he is spending your eight thousand pounds.[30]

O'Connell's brother James came to his help in raising money to pay O'Leary's creditors. O'Connell was forced to borrow £3,600 from John Hickson of College Green, Dublin, on what James called 'unfair and usurious terms'.[31] Having signed a deed pledging his own property James wrote his brother a lecture:

> You will have this *precious deed* by Thursday morning and I sin-cerely hope it will be the means of saving you from destruction whatever my fate may be, but now *that the die is cast* I can with truth say that I am by being made a party to this business exquisitely miserable as I am no longer master of my own or of the very limited property I inherited in right of my father. We both are at the mercy of the men in the world I detest most, and should this affair come to the knowledge of my Uncle Maurice [Hunting-Cap], I am convinced he will never give me a guinea. . . . I was well aware when I affixed my name to this accursed deed that in all human probability my prospects in life were for ever blasted . . . though by the contents of your letters you seem to think that I have the egregious folly to suppose I am only doing a mere act of courtesy. I now conclude this to me most disagreeable subject by saying you have involved me in the ruin you have been so long preparing for your amiable wife and interesting family.[32]

It was of course vital that Hunting-Cap should not discover that O'Connell was involved in O'Leary's bankruptcy, all the more so since, as he told James, he had warned his nephew to have nothing to do with O'Leary. The old man questioned James closely and only desisted when

James solemnly assured him that his brother 'would not lose a guinea by the fellow'. In telling O'Connell of this James added that their sister Ellen was assisting their efforts to prevent the news from reaching Hunting-Cap:

> She had two confidential men stationed, one at the upper gate and the other at the strand, to caution every person who was coming to Derrynane not to mention this business. This, I assure you, was a very necessary caution as every individual in this country knows every circumstance connected with O'Leary's failure.[33]

It was typical of O'Connell's buoyant temperament that he should have adopted a confident attitude to his troubles, and he informed his wife from Limerick:

> Bad as the circuit has been I have already received or carried upwards of 200 guineas so that, darling, with health, spirits and the assistance of God, we will work over the difficulties into which my most absurd credulity involved me. Dearest, sweetest, how I *ought* to love you for the manner in which you have met those difficulties.[34]

One ray of light was the generosity of Count O'Connell, who came to his nephew's aid by lending him £3,600 to pay off the loan from John Hickson.[35]

In March 1817, in response to one of O'Connell's many requests for loans and assistance in raising loans, James enclosed a list he had just drawn up of his brother's debts. They amounted to £18,699, but James felt that the list was not complete and that the grand total would be more than £20,000. The list included the debt of £3,600 to Count O'Connell, as already mentioned, £2,274 to Denys Scully, a total of at least £3,000 'in Iveragh to common men', and small amounts to a dozen relatives including £100 to O'Connell's own mother and £130 to Hunting-Cap's clerk, and £2,000 to James O'Leary's creditors.[36] Of Count O'Connell's loan of £3,600 none of the principal was repaid and only a small part of the interest. In December 1821 the count came to grips with reality and made his nephew a gift of the loan.[37]

Mary O'Connell had always acted as an informal financial agent for her husband when he was away on the Munster circuit. He would send her money for household expenses, for placing to his account in a bank, and for meeting the many bills of exchange which he had accepted. His indebtedness had reached a disastrous point by the spring of 1822 and his letters to his wife contained dozens of instructions. His letter of 8 April shows the critical state of his finances:

I perceive by a letter I got last night from James Sugrue that Dr Wilson's bill lies over unpaid. Let it be so, darling, for a few days longer. You have therefore got from me in half-notes between you and James Sugrue £200 and he has got £100 from Roger so that, as you gave him the other £50, you will have only to add £12 10s. to it. Then, giving your mother £15 you will still have £172 10s. in hands. Take out of that £42 10s. for house expenses, it will leave you £130 out of which you will, before this reaches you, pay tomorrow £40, Eyre's bill, and the day you get this £50, Higgins's bill, and you will have £40 towards meeting the bills due on Thursday. I believe my letter of yesterday was erroneous in supposing that Eyre's £40 would not be due until Wednesday. I hope this error will not occasion a protest, as in the list I sent I marked down a £40 bill as due the 9th. I will, please God, send you a banker's bill for at least £200. The bills which are to be paid are 9th, £40 to Eyre, 10th, £50 to Higgins, 11th, £58 *with interest* to Mr Mahon — same day, 11th — £138 10s. to Dr Wilson, a *fresh* bill not the one already due, 15th, £69 19*s*. to Roose, 25th, £75 Clongowes Wood College payable, I think, to Elliot, 28th, £50 to Cooper.[38]

But Mary fell down on the job: about a week previous to the sending of this list of instructions she paid the wrong bill of exchange, thus jeopardising her husband's complicated credit system. O'Connell must have sent her a stern reprimand, because on the following day he tried to undo its effect:

Will you, can you forgive me for the cruel and ferocious letter I wrote you, my darling heart, last night. . . . The fact is just this, my own love, that I am greatly pressed for money this month. I never in my life was so much so. . . . My letter was to be sure a barbarous one unbecoming a gentleman or a Christian, but it gives you an opportunity of behaving generously to me in return and I know my love too well not to be sure you will do what is generous. We are nearly twenty years married, darling, and this is my *first offence*. It shall, I hope, sweetest, be my last. I wish I were near you to pat your cheek and press your sweet lips as a seal to my forgiveness.[39]

He was forgiven. A few days later he wrote again to her:

If you had a mind, my darling heart's love, to wring your husband's very soul you could not have done it more effectually than by writing the sweet, gentle, uncomplaining letter I got from you last night. Oh, how could I be so base as to write such a letter as I did to such a woman! ... It was this disposition of yours, Mary, that fascinated me in early life and that made me continue your lover for twenty years after I became your husband.[40]

There was a serious famine in Ireland in 1822 and the barony of Iveragh was hard hit. By the early spring of that year O'Connell knew that he must expect a sharp fall in his rents.[41] This knowledge may well have been the deciding factor in persuading him and his wife that the only way out of their difficulties was to adopt a policy of rigid economy. It was arranged that Mary and the five youngest of their seven children should live abroad cheaply, while the house in Merrion Square should be let or at least have its establishment reduced, the carriage and the horses sold.[42] On 2 May 1822 they sailed from Dublin for Bordeaux. Finding the summer climate in Pau, their first place of residence, too unpleasant they moved to Tours where they stayed twelve months. After a sojourn in Paris they settled in Southampton in the autumn of 1823 and returned to Dublin in May 1824, having been altogether two years abroad.

In his letters to his wife in France, O'Connell accused himself repeatedly of being responsible for their separation. Two days after her departure he wrote:

My love, do you not now reproach that loose and profligate waste of money to many and many an ungrateful and undeserving object which makes it necessary for us to separate. No, my love, you do not reproach it but my own heart does, and the misery I now endure is nothing but the punishment I deserve for not being more attentive.[43]

And again, two weeks later:

How miserable I am! What a vile wretch! It was for my own follies and idle gratifications that I made it necessary to separate from you and my children. I deserve the punishment.[44]

But Mary's reply was consoling:

You are, heart, much more religious than your Mary, and from the moment it was deemed necessary for me to come with my family to France, I put on the resolution to bear it like a Christian. Do not, my own love, make me unhappy by those reproaches you cast on your-self. You never deserved any from me. You have been the best and most beloved of husbands and you will continue such to the last hour of my life.[45]

O'Connell's brother, James, to whom a policy of thrift was one of the pleasures of life, approved of the decision to go abroad and used it to deliver another lecture:

> It is, I am convinced, absolutely necessary you should at once diminish your establishment. . . . Whether you will better your situation much by taking J[ames] Connor's house and fixing yourself in Tralee where *you must keep an open house for all your family*, I will not attempt to decide, but I trust you have made your entire family acquainted with your real situation. If they and you are serious in wishing to conform yourselves to your embarrassed circumstances, the south of France would in my opinion be the place to fix them.[46]

Unfortunately the saving of money — if saving there was — by the enforced separation does not appear to have effected any improvement in O'Connell's financial position. In September 1823 he appealed to James for a new loan but his request was refused and with a customary reprimand:

> When you talk of the security afforded by the conveying your property to me for any money I may advance, do you forget that your present debts amount at least to double the value of your life use of it and, as to the plan of economy adopted by you with respect to your family, it is indeed a very novel one. In the course of a few months they move from Dublin to Pau, from that to Tours, now they are in the most expensive part of Paris and will wind up by fixing their residence in England, the dearest country in Europe to live in. . . . The resources of your profession are enormous if not squandered or dissipated.[47]

Three days later James wrote again

> I this evening received your voluminous letter of the 9th inst. and now for *the third and last time most solemnly declare* I will not give you the small sum I have in the funds. . . . You have ever been a most affectionate brother and indeed we had a right to be proud of you. We both [James and his brother John] cheerfully gave you £1,700 of our share of the General's [Count O'Connell's] money seven years ago . . . *but since that period to this hour we did not receive one shilling principal or interest.* . . . There is no instance of a man who ruined and dissipated his own and his children's property, having too scrupulous a regard for the interests of those who have not such strong claims on him. I will not attempt to conceal from you the danger to

you and your family should my poor uncle [Hunting-Cap] hear of your embarrassments.[48]

To this warning James added the frightening statement that 'you will be most fortunate if means are had to enable you to resume your professional avocations in Dublin next month' — a reference to the possibility of O'Connell's being committed to a debtors' prison. However the worried but affectionate James came to his brother's rescue by going security for a further loan but this one would be the last:

> I have *on my knees bound myself by an oath, during the rest of my life never again to join you in bill, bond or note or in any other security, either verbal or otherwise, for one guinea, and further I have solemnly sworn on my knees never to give you in any one year during my life any sum of money exceeding twenty pounds. This oath I have taken without any evasion, equivocation or mental reservation.*[49]

To this undertaking James added the comment, 'it is an insult on commonsense to have you talk of the security you can offer for money'. In the same letter he returned to his earlier warning: 'as to your profession, surely ill-health or arrest for debt would completely knock you up? Two months later James advised his brother to insist on his family's living in one place permanently and added,

> Their tour to the Continent, which was intended to be of use to your finances, has beyond all doubt contributed to add largely to your debts. This however is a subject I will never again renew. If what you have suffered heretofore by your waste of money has not cured you, anything I could say would of course make no impression.[50]

A few days later O'Connell received a friendly but pressing letter from the rector of Clongowes Wood College, the celebrated Fr Peter Kenney, S.J. Out of gratitude to their father, who was serving under Bolivar in South America, O'Connell had taken a personal interest in the education of two boys, Alexander and John Burke of Clonmel. Their fees had not been paid for over a year, and Fr Kenney was becoming restive; 'the difficulty of getting in debts long due to this house makes the charge of providing for this large establishment a very arduous undertaking. I should feel particularly obliged by a line from you on the subject'.[51] Denys Scully, a leading figure in the emancipation movement, was demanding the return of £2,000 which O'Connell had promised to repay within six months but the six months had elongated to eight years: 'try and stir yourself and endeavour to get rid of this engagement without delay'.[52]

To her husband's suggestion that the family should return to live in a rural part of Ireland Mary returned a firm answer. Dublin was the only part of Ireland not injurious to her health. Living in any other part of the country she would be too ill to care for her family, and 'in a bed of sickness how could I enjoy your society?' There could be no economy in living in Kerry: 'your doors could not be kept shut to your connections or to mine. There would be an eternal *relay of cousins.*'[53]

A major objection to returning concerned their daughters:

> The society of a country town in Ireland is not the most advantageous for young girls educated as they have been. . . . [James's] or John's family could live in any place or in any way they liked, but you have a respectability to keep up for yours which it is impossible to have until you are out of your difficulties and able to have them, as they ought to be, in Dublin. The world is unkind and *they* would delight to think your embarrassments were such as to oblige you to send your family to live separate from you in the same kingdom.[54]

But a week later Mary changed her mind and decided on the return to Ireland.[55] Her decision was greeted by her husband with the words, 'never was blooming bride so welcome to her husband's arms as my own, own Mary to mine'.[56] She made the stipulation that life in Merrion Square must be on a reduced scale — at most, four domestic servants, no carriage and no horses.[57] Part of her reluctance to return had been due, she told her husband, to a promise she had given to Count O'Connell not to go back until all the debts had been paid.[58] Three months later, in May 1824, the family arrived home.

The fact that O'Connell expected to receive a large bequest from Hunting-Cap was a major reason for his extravagance. On one occasion he told his wife, 'I always looked to the resources to come from my Uncle Maurice's succession as the means of paying off and I went in debt on that speculation'.[59] He had probably expected Hunting-Cap to live to a ripe old age but not to survive into his ninety-seventh year.

Relief came at long last with the death of the old man in February 1825. Apart from land, Hunting-Cap left £52,000 in cash, mortgages, arrears of rent, livestock, furniture and other assets.[60] This sum was divided equally between O'Connell and his two brothers, John and James.[61] The arrears of rent were calculated at £8,000 at least, but the brothers agreed to remit the bulk of them and collect only £2,500.[62] Of the £52,000 less the amount of arrears remitted, O'Connell received about £15,000.[63] This enabled him to pay most of his debts and to obtain a lower rate of interest from his remaining creditors.[64]

Now that Hunting-Cap was dead O'Connell's income from land amounted to about £4,000 a year, taking into account also what he had obtained from his father.[65] The ultimate result of his impecunious marriage was that he shared Hunting-Cap's wealth with his two brothers — each receiving about a third — instead of being the sole or at least the principal heir. An error frequently appearing in books on O'Connell is the statement that he inherited an estate with a rental of £1,000. This confusion may well have arisen from his own statement that he had inherited *hereditary* property of that income.[66] By this he would have meant land in the continued possession of his family since the seventeenth century or earlier.

The death of Hunting-Cap however did not bring an end to financial anxiety. In 1826 Count O'Connell expressed his disappointment that the total of £20,000 which, he said, his nephew had received from Hunting-Cap and himself had not sufficed to 'expunge the enormous mass of your debts'. He proposed that O'Connell should insure his life for £10,000 so that, when he died, this sum could be divided among his three younger sons:

One thing however enforces itself on my mind, namely, that the progress of years will disable you from pursuing your professional labours, and that the fate, nay the very existence, of your large family hangs on your life. I am therefore impelled . . . to urge the following proposal which, by securing an independence to your three young sons, will have the effect of setting your mind at rest as far as regards them and of enabling you to apply your savings from your large income to the extinguishment of any remaining debts and establishing your two unmarried daughters.[67]

The annual premium would be £482. 10s. and the Count offered to pay a third of this.[68] O'Connell does not appear to have accepted this proposal and, perhaps, wisely. James considered the premium too high since 'you, I thank God, are as likely to live many years as any person of your age in Ireland'.[69] Count O'Connell had for some time been sending James money, saved as a result of his own policy of rigid economy,[70] to invest as a trust fund for O'Connell's younger sons. By March 1827 this sum amounted to £1,500.[71] When O'Connell sought to obtain it, James was adamant. He could not give it to him 'without a breach of a most solemn promise I made our uncle'.[72]

In July 1825 O'Connell's eldest daughter, Ellen, married Christopher Fitz-Simon and received a dowry of £5,000. This sum was paid — as one might expect — on the instalment plan, being spread over the four years 1825 to 1829.[73] As soon as he had inherited Derrynane from Hunting-Cap

in 1825 O'Connell set about making improvements, and he extended the
house by the addition of four reception rooms and some bedrooms, turning
the back of the house into the front. The cost was greater than he had
anticipated.[74] An additional cause of anxiety was the loss of professional
income suffered in 1825 when he was in London in connection with the
emancipation bill of that year. He estimated that his sojourn there had
altogether cost him over £3,000, travelling and hotel expenses being no
doubt included in that figure.[75]

To meet his continuing state of indebtedness he seems to have worked
even harder at the bar. In 1827 he told his wife that he had received £738
in fees during November, £50 or £60 more than he had ever previously
earned in one month, even though legal business in general was slack.[76]
A few days later he wrote: 'my income is now a fine one, upwards of
£7,000 a year, but it is run away with by debts and engagements'.[77] This
figure must have been calculated by him on the money earned in a short
period, since his fee book notes his earnings at £4,868 in 1827 and £5,178
in 1828.[78] Possibly his fee book did not register the entire of his professional income.

The many instances of expenditure already described prove that
O'Connell was naturally extravagant — in gifts and loans to friends, in
going security, in that soft and facile disposition of which Hunting-Cap
complained, and perhaps in not attempting to keep his family on a tighter
rein. Their changes of residence during their two years abroad suggest a
lack of determination to live cheaply. When they had been about to leave
for France O'Connell told his wife how pleased James was to hear of their
plans, but 'all he fears as usual is that they will not practise economy there
for want of *skill* in that art'.[79] Some weeks after her arrival in France he
wrote; 'be, darling, like me in love with every farthing because the pence
saved will hurry the reunion of our family. . . . I suppose, darling, you keep
an accurate account of every *cent* you pay'.[80] A few days later he again
advised her to be 'as penurious as you can'.[81] For O'Connell to counsel
thrift sounds like colossal cheek but the fact that he made these pleas at
all (while accusing himself of being the essential cause of their separation)
suggests that Mary was not of a thrifty disposition. Perhaps she knew from
long experience that a parsimonious wife would only irritate her husband
and that his expenditure would always exceed his income. She may well
have got out of the habit of thrift.

From 1825, when he inherited Derrynane, O'Connell resided there for
about six weeks every autumn. Many travellers have testified to the fact
that he kept open house and welcomed all to his table. One may presume
that a liberal hospitality was also dispensed at his house in Merrion Square.
There is little mention of this in his correspondence and, naturally enough,

virtually none in the journals of tourists; visits to town houses do not provide travellers with tales. Letters between O'Connell and his wife were written when he was away from home, and convention did not encourage nineteenth-century wives to entertain liberally when their husbands were absent. However, on two occasions Mary's letters contain illuminating comments. In 1819 she and her children were spending the summer in a house outside Dublin, and she wrote to her husband:

> I assure you, love, this house often reminds me of what Carhen [the home of O'Connell parents] was. Not a week passes without visitors of some kind. Maurice [O'Connell's eldest son], just like yourself and your poor father, cannot see any friend without asking them to spend a day or two in the country with him.[82]

Carhen was in a remote part of the world, and visitors would have been very few: Merrion Square was in the heart of Dublin and, because of O'Connell's political position, 'friends' would have been legion. The second occasion was in 1825, shortly after Ellen's marriage, when thoughts were being directed to marrying off the second daughter, Kate: 'If we are, darling, obliged to give a dinner and a ball to great folks, let us not ask as many folk of the other description as we have been in the habit of asking'.[83] The implication in both letters is that hospitality was dispensed freely and without very much discrimination.

Donations to charity — private and institutional — had always been part of his regular expenditure. Mary's concern over his distribution of money whenever he visited Kerry has already been noted. In 1822 James wrote:

> Your income from lands is so cut up by interest of money, annuities to poor relations and to fosterers, so that, in the best of times, you have but little to *actually touch*.[84]

O'Connell had been fostered out, and in accordance with the old Gaelic tradition a man was expected to treat his foster relatives with affection. The newspaper lists of donations show that he subscribed liberally to charitable institutions. In 1840 the Presentation Sisters settled at Cahirciveen and opened a school. He presented them with a dwelling house and ground for the school, some furniture including a piano, and a small estate some miles outside the town producing a net rental of £70.[85] When Edmund Ignatius Rice, the founder of the Irish Christian Brothers, told him of a grave shortage of funds in connection with their school at Hanover St., Dublin, O'Connell replied: 'put me down for one thousand pounds'. But Rice refused the proffered sum, knowing — as Rice's biographer tactfully observed — 'the many demands on the Liberator's purse'.[86] Rice was a realist. A gift of land in Kerry was one thing: trying to find £1,000 in cash was quite another.

Immediately after the passing of the catholic emancipation act in 1829 a national testimonium was organised and presented to O'Connell in recognition of his services. The amount he received must have been very considerable, perhaps as much as £20,000,[87] and must certainly have enabled him to pay all his debts. He now gave up his practice at the bar and applied himself wholly to politics. He was faced with the considerable expense of living in London for much of the year in order to attend parliament, and of trying to maintain some new kind of political organisation now that the Catholic Association had come to an end. To compensate him for his loss of professional income and to meet these new expenses an annual collection was inaugurated, known as the O'Connell tribute or rent. In the years after 1829 he made occasional references to indebtedness, but in May 1846 congratulated himself on having reduced his bank overdraft to £4,000.[88]

O'Connell appears to have sold some of the land he had received from Hunting-Cap, since he passed on to his eldest son Maurice only the *entailed* estate which, as already stated, had a net rent in 1848 of some £2,600. In addition however he left a small property at Drumquinna, near Kenmare, County Kerry, worth about £400 a year, which he had purchased from the McSwiney family into which his sister Brigid had married. It was subject, however, to life annuities amounting to £130 a year.[89] In 1826 he had bought his mother's family property at Brittas, near Mallow, County Cork, for £3,200. It had a net rental of some £400 but was subject to life annuities payable to members of his mother's family, the O'Mullanes. On some occasion before his death he settled this property on his second son Morgan.[90]

In his will O'Connell bequeathed £1,000 (later reduced by a codicil to £630) to the Repeal Association:

> I implore that it may be received by a vote of the committee and afterwards of the Repeal Association itself as in full satisfaction of any demand that body may or could have upon me. In short that if more be in anywise due of me that it may be fully and freely remitted to me so as to leave no kind of debt to the association weighing on my soul.[91]

To this will, executed in October 1846, he added six codicils, two of them in one day, 12 March 1847, which suggest the fretful state of his mind. He bequeathed £8,000 to his daughters Kate (Mrs Charles O'Connell) and Betsey (Mrs Nicholas Ffrench) and his sons John and Daniel. Since his debts were considerable it is doubtful if they received anything like the whole of this sum.[92] Owing to the famine, rents fell heavily into arrear so that the financial position of Maurice, his heir, confronted by O'Connell's debts, by head rents and other encumbrances, was far from secure. The position was made worse by Maurice's own tendency to be extravagant and by his neglect for some time to appreciate the seriousness of the situation.[93] To meet the debts and whatever proportion of the legacies that could be paid, the executors — O'Connell's sons, Maurice, Morgan and John — were forced to sell the house in Merrion Square together with its furniture and library, and the library and, probably, most of the furniture in Derrynane.[94] Silver and other objects presented to O'Connell were retained by the family.

O'Connell was fortunate in having as attorney his old friend and political colleague, Pierce Mahony. Though a Protestant, Mahony had been the parliamentary agent in London of the Catholic Association in the critical period leading up to the passing of the emancipation act in 1829. It was obviously due to his careful and tactful handling of affairs that Maurice O'Connell was able to retain possession of Derrynane after his father's death.

2

Religious freedom

The declaration of the Second Vatican Council on Religious Freedom
has borne witness to the success of a movement that had been in
existence for a century and a half. This declaration gave expression to the
principle that every man has the right to worship God publicly according
to his conscience, to propagate his religious beliefs and to be free from
discrimination on account of those beliefs. However, this principle had
received practical recognition in many parts of the Christian world long
before Vatican II. In the United States of America religious freedom had
existed since the early days of independence. It was therefore only natural
that the American Church should have taken a leading part in the Council's
deliberations.

But the assertion of this principle was not confined to the American
Church nor did it find its roots only in America. In Europe also, ideas of
religious freedom and equality and their corollary, separation of church
and state,[1] found supporters in the early nineteenth century.

The first European Catholic, and perhaps even the first prominent
political figure in any of the major Christian denominations[2] in Europe, to
espouse these ideas was Daniel O'Connell.[3] He was followed some fifteen
years later by the French Liberal Catholics, Lamennais, Lacordaire and
the young Montalembert, and by the Italian priest, Gioacchino Ventura.
Admittedly, many Europeans from the time of Voltaire had expressed
support for religious freedom but their views were usually coloured by
indifference or hostility to religion itself or at least to one or other of the
Christian churches. The special importance of O'Connell and the Continental Liberal Catholics in this context arose from the fact that they were
practising Catholics.

Some Catholic churchmen in Austria at the time of Joseph II favoured
a major degree of religious freedom and equality, but subject to a system
of state regulation[4] which O'Connell and the Liberal Catholics would have
found wholly unacceptable.

Much has been written on O'Connell and religious freedom but no attempt has been made to state clearly what his views were or to indicate how radical they were. One obvious reason for this is that none of his biographers undertook a comprehensive investigation of his career. Furthermore, on this subject they concentrated their interest on his role in the Veto controversy which arose from the attempt by the British Government to obtain from Rome a right of veto in the nomination of bishops. This controversy involved major issues — relations between the Catholic Church and a Protestant government, between the Papacy and a local church, and between the Papacy and a local laity (since the Irish bishops were divided on the subject) — but it did not extend to religious freedom in the most fundamental sense as dealt with by Vatican II. Finally, virtually all his biographers lived in the English-speaking political world and were not directly concerned with the quarrel between Rome and Liberalism which was a major practical problem only in those countries where Catholicism was the established religion.

In order to understand the radical nature of O'Connell's views it is necessary to consider what the orthodox view was in his time. Briefly stated in practical terms, it was that a Catholic government must assist and protect the Church and its teaching and must not allow (except for reasons of prudence) the propagation of contrary doctrines. This teaching was confirmed by Gregory XVI's encyclical, *Mirari vos*, in 1832, Pius IX's *Syllabus of Errors* in 1864 and Leo XIII's *Immortale Dei* in 1885. These Papal documents condemned the principle, but not necessarily the practice, of religious freedom. As the nineteenth century neared its end the Church had come to accept the practice of this freedom in most predominantly Catholic countries, either from necessity as in France and Italy or because of the gradual adoption of Liberal political attitudes as in the Austrian Empire. But the condemnation of the principle of religious freedom remained part of official teaching until Vatican II. That council did not attempt to refute the principles on which this teaching rested. Instead, it broke new ground by resting its concept of religious freedom on the natural rights of persons and groups, rights logically anterior to the principles on which the former teaching was based.

In order to gain some understanding of O'Connell's views it is necessary to consider first the Ireland into which he was born. That Ireland was officially a Protestant state in which the (Anglican) Church of Ireland was established and in which Catholics were barred from government office and from admission to parliament. The position of the subject Catholic population was complicated by the fact that after the Williamite conquest the Papacy continued to recognise the exiled Stuarts as the legitimate sovereigns of Great Britain and Ireland. This involved allowing the Stuart kings the right to nominate to vacant Irish bishoprics. The recognition bore heavily on the Catholics since it laid them open to the charge of political disloyalty and served as an argument in favour of the retention of the Penal Laws. Paradoxically, the Catholic Church in Ireland through the eighteenth century enjoyed a greater freedom from government interference (the exiled Stuarts having no political power) than was the case in nearly all other European countries. But by the time that the titular James III died in 1766 it was clear that all hope of a Stuart restoration had vanished, and the Papacy refrained from recognising the claims of his son, Charles III (Bonnie Prince Charlie). Henceforth, complete separation of church and state was a fact in Catholic Ireland.

Realising that there could be no hope of having the Penal Laws repealed until Catholics formally declared their unequivocal loyalty to the British sovereign, the Catholic Committee — a body of landowners and merchants of a loosely representative character — were most anxious that the Irish Parliament should pass an act providing an oath of political allegiance which would enable Catholics to qualify as loyal subjects. In 1774 such an oath was enacted but it contained several phrases — most of them implicitly insulting to the Papacy — which many Catholics found unacceptable. A number of prominent laymen and some of the bishops took the oath but other bishops refused and sought a formal condemnation from Rome. Though expressing strong disapproval of the oath Rome refrained from condemning it. For a time the Catholic Committee was disturbed by the division between 'jurors' and 'non-jurors', but by 1778 virtually all opposition to the taking of the oath was abandoned.[5]

These events and the whole Irish situation meant that Daniel O'Connell was born into a Catholic society accustomed to complete separation of church and state and one in which church-state issues and the distinction between spiritual and political allegiances had been vigorously debated. Moreover, it was a society which had seen a church-state link (the continued Papal recognition of the exiled Stuarts) as inimical to the welfare of a people. He was clearly 'conditioned' by his Irish environment to be sceptical of the value of traditional beliefs in regard to church-state relations.

One must also consider O'Connell's education and early manhood. He received his first schooling at home in Kerry and then in a school near Cobh, Co. Cork. When fourteen he was sent to the Continent to St Omer and then to the English College at Douai. It was natural that he should go to France since his family had maintained intimate relations with that country through the eighteenth century: just before the Revolution he had more than a dozen relatives holding commissions in the French army. But the college at Douai was closed by the Revolutionary Government in January, 1793, and O'Connell and his fellow students were forced to leave

France like refugees.

As a law student in the 1790s, first in London and then in Dublin, O'Connell became a rationalist[6] and remained one for perhaps a decade. Some years after settling into legal practice in Ireland and after his marriage he recovered his religious belief[7] and remained a convinced Catholic for the rest of his life. His study of the writings of the *philosophes* and, in particular, of the English radicals Paine and Godwin, must have encouraged him to see the French Revolution in a new light and to adopt many of its principles as his own. The rationalist interlude no doubt gave him an insight into religious freedom and a desire to make it part of his recovered religious belief.

In his early manhood O'Connell's closest companions would have been law students and young barristers. A gregarious type, he made friends and acquaintances readily, and he would obviously have been influenced by his colleagues. In fact there is positive evidence that this was the case.[8] The vast majority of these young men were Protestants,[9] and he was a particularly close friend of a young Protestant barrister, Richard Newton Bennett.[10] O'Connell was thus intimate with views and principles very different from those he had known in earlier life. Protestants were no more sympathetic to religious freedom than Catholics but these differing influences may well have encouraged a young man who was a rationalist to adopt the principle of religious freedom all the more readily.

An indication of the way his mind was developing can be seen in an entry he made in his journal in 1797:

> Why should truth be so disagreeable to the human ear? Is it that her light would dazzle? No. Persecution springs from self-love. Those who do not pay the tribute of coincidence to our decisions become our most hated foes.[11]

O'Connell is known to have commenced his long struggle for Catholic Emancipation as early as November, 1804.[12] Whether he had as yet returned to his religious belief one cannot say, but family tradition as well as his rationalism — assuming he still retained it — would have been sufficient to induce him to seek freedom and equality for his Catholic countrymen. He is first known to have propounded his unorthodox views on religious freedom at a meeting of Catholics in Dublin in 1807 when he said that he would place the Catholic claims 'on the new score of justice — of that justice which would emancipate the Protestant in Spain and Portugal, the Christian in Constantinople.'[13] In a speech in Dublin in 1813 he elaborated further:

There can be no freedom without perfect liberty of conscience. . . . The emancipation I look for is one which would establish the rights of conscience upon a general principle . . . which would serve and liberate the Catholic in Ireland but would be equally useful to the Protestant in Spain . . . which would destroy the Inquisition and the Protestant Orange lodges together, and have no sacrilegious intruder between man and his Creator. I esteem the Roman Catholic religion as the most eligible. All I require is that the [Anglican] Protestant, the Presbyterian, the Dissenter, the Methodist. should pay the same compliment to his own persuasion and leave its success to its own persuasive powers without calling in the profane assistance of temporal terrors or the corrupt influence of temporal rewards.[14]

Five years later, at a public dinner in Tralee, Co. Kerry he said:

My political creed is short and simple. It consists in believing that all men are entitled as of right and justice to religious and civil liberty. I deserve no credit for being the advocate of religious liberty as my wants alone require such advocacy; but I have taken care to require it only on that principle which would equally grant it to all sects and persuasions which, while it emancipated the Catholic in Ireland, would protect the Protestant in France and Italy and destroy the Inquisition, together with the inquisitors, in Spain. Religion is debased and degraded by human interference; and surely the worship of the Deity cannot but be contaminated by the admixture of worldly ambition or human force.[15]

In the years between 1818 and the successful conclusion of the campaign for Catholic Emancipation in 1829 O'Connell does not seem to have made any further striking statements on religious freedom. Shortly after the Emancipation Act was passed, however, he wrote an important letter to Isaac Lyon Goldsmid, the political leader of British Jews, on the subject of their emancipation. In this letter he offered them his active support, and advised:

Do not listen to those over-cautious persons who may recommend postponement. Believe an agitator of some experience that nothing was ever obtained by delay — at least in politics. You must to a certain extent force your claims on the parliament. You cannot be worse, recollect, even by a failure and you ought to be the better by the experiment.[16]

Of vital interest to the subject of religious freedom is the passage:

> I entirely agree with you on the principle of freedom of conscience, and no man can admit that sacred principle without extending it equally to the Jew as to the Christian. To my mind it is an eternal and universal truth that we are responsible to God alone for our religious belief and that human laws are impious when they attempt to control the exercise of those acts of individual or general devotion which such belief requires. I think not lightly of the awful responsibility of rejecting *true belief* but that responsibility is entirely between man and his creator, and any fellow being who usurps dominion over belief is to my mind a blasphemer against the deity as he certainly is a tyrant over his fellow creatures.

On the subject of separation of church and state O'Connell's views were equally unorthodox for a practising Catholic in his day. He made his first major statement in this context in 1830 on the French Revolution of that year. That revolution overthrew the intransigently Catholic government of Charles X and substituted for it the Liberal and anti-clerical regime of Louis-Philippe. In Dublin a month later O'Connell's son-in-law, Christopher Fitz-Simon, and financial agent, P. V. FitzPatrick, organized a meeting in honour of the revolution. On holiday at Derrynane, his home in Co. Kerry, O'Connell was unable to attend, but he wrote a public letter which was read to the meeting. He erroneously thought that the new government would break the connection between it and the Catholic Church, and he hailed it accordingly. The following passage occurred in his letter:

> The French Revolution is in all its aspects consolatory and deserving of the highest praise. . . . There is one feature in this great and satisfactory change which I hail with the most profound conviction of utility — the complete severance of the church from the state. Infidelity . . . which has deluged France with the blood of the Catholic clergy, was losing ground by degrees since the concordat obtained by Napoleon; but the progress of Christian truth and of genuine piety was much impeded since the return of the Bourbons by the un-hallowed commixture of zeal for religion with servile attachment to the Bourbons. . . . The Catholic clergy of France are learned, pious, exemplary and most charitable and zealous. But they were placed in a false position. The events of the first revolution, written in characters of blood, convinced them that the safety of religion was connected with the security of the throne. . . . I heartily rejoice that

the last revolution has altered the position. . . . Religion has regained its natural station.[17]

The revolution in France encouraged outbreaks of a Liberal and nationalist kind in other parts of Europe. One of these occurred in the Papal States where in February 1831 a provisional government was set up which decreed the abolition of the temporal power of the Pope. O'Connell hailed these events in a speech made to a public dinner in London:

Revolution was now spreading in Italy, and that beautiful country was at length about to assert its rights. He trusted that the period was not far distant when the Church there would be separated from the state, for in every country that appeared to him an adulterous connection.[18]

An even more decided approval of separation of church and state was expressed by O'Connell in 1837 in two debates in the House of Commons on British policy in regard to the civil war then raging in Spain between the 'traditionalist' forces of Don Carlos and the 'Liberal' supporters of Queen Isabella. He saw the struggle as between despotism and liberty (though later events suggest that his interpretation of Spanish affairs was over-simplified), and in consequence supported the British Foreign Secretary, Lord Palmerston, who had given informal sanction to the forces of Isabella. In one of his two speeches O'Connell warned the House that victory for Don Carlos would mean the restoration of the 'hateful inquisition' and the reestablishment of 'that disastrous connection between church and state which for nearly two centuries has plunged Spain into the deepest moral degradation.'[19] In his other address on the Spanish war he said:

The period is fast advancing upon us (and I know that, at Rome, its approach is hailed with joy) at which the unholy union of church and state will be permanently severed in all countries professing the Catholic religion — to the securing, I am confident, the purity of the one and the consolidating the safety of the other.[20]

It is likely that O'Connell's views provoked strong feelings in Rome, especially now that he had attacked the church-state position in Spain in such an important forum as the English House of Commons. In this regard there is some interesting information in a short biography of O'Connell by Jules Gondon, the French Catholic journalist.[21] According to Gondon, unjust and calumnious press accounts of O'Connell's religious orthodoxy had produced such an effect in Rome that in 1837 the Pope, Gregory XVI, refused him the privilege of a portable altar.[22] The friend, who had undertaken the task of obtaining the privilege, did not dare tell O'Connell that it had been refused. Instead, he informed him that newspapers had from time to time attributed such strange language to him that Rome did not know what to think on the matter of his orthodoxy. O'Connell sought to remove these suspicions by writing his friend in Rome a letter which included the passage:

> I revere in all things the authority of the Holy See. I really believe (in so far as I know myself) that there is not a single person who pays more sincerely than I do, and with all my heart, that submission — in the widest sense of the word — to the Holy See which the Catholic Church demands of her children. I have never said and shall never say a single word which I would not subject to her authority with profound obedience. I am attached to the centre of unity with the most ardent desire never to separate myself from it either in thought or word or action, and if I should ever deceive myself in the opinion[s], I express I hope that they will be interpreted according to my sentiments because my submission to the authority of the Church is complete, whole and universal.[23]

Gondon adds that these lines were brought to the notice of Gregory who, in consequence, granted the privilege sought.[24]

Despite his divergence from the official doctrine on religious freedom and separation of church and state O'Connell was a very zealous layman in many fields — defence of the poorer Catholics against the proselytising efforts of evangelical Protestants; support of the establishment of Catholic schools, notably by the newly formed Irish Christian Brothers; and engagement in public debate on behalf of the Church's position in certain matters.

Because of his interest in polemics he cooperated with Rev. Nicholas (later Cardinal) Wiseman and the Irish journalist, Michael J. Quin, in launching the *Dublin Review* in 1836. It was a quarterly designed to provide a platform for Catholic writers on general topics and religious debate, a Catholic counterpart to the two *de facto* Protestant quarterlies, the Whig *Edinburgh Review* and the Tory *Quarterly Review*.

When Quin withdrew from the post of editor after the first two numbers O'Connell received an application for the vacancy from the able William Howitt, a Quaker. He favored Howitt's appointment but left the final decision on the matter to Wiseman. He pointed out to the latter that should Howitt be appointed it would be necessary to have a Catholic examine all articles before publication. O'Connell went on to say that he himself could not perform that function, partly because he resided in Dublin (the periodical was being published in London) but also because 'I go farther than you would probably approve upon the topic of separation of the church from the state' and thus 'I am unfit to be the censor of our press so as to have your confidence.'[25]

In telling Howitt that he favoured his application O'Connell expressed himself candidly on the religious nature of the review and on his own conception of religious freedom:

> The *Dublin Review* is a Catholic publication, emphatically Catholic — I should say, rather polemically so. This is quite consistent with its advocacy of the principles of civil as well as religious freedom, that is, the perfect freedom from penal laws, tests or legal restrictions, the separation, in short, of the kingdom of God from the kingdom of Caesar. But in point of religion it must advocate the truth of Catholic doctrines exclusively. I need not tell you that that is my own conviction. My firm belief is that the duty of every man is to be a Catholic whilst I abhor every attempt either by direct penalty or by any civil exclusion to bring the law in any way in aid of my creed. I am indeed unequivocally *a voluntary*.[26]

O'Connell made another notable statement on these matters in 1842 in the course of a public controversy with Lord Shrewsbury, the aristocratic leader of the English Catholics. Though the debate dealt primarily with political topics he saw fit to reprove Shrewsbury for having an inadequate concept of religious freedom, and went on to say:

> With a popular government private morality is under the guard of public opinion. . . . It is to the Church — to the Catholic Church — that the honest spirit of democracy ought to be, and must be, the most useful. The respect which each person would claim for his own opinion would require of him to treat with equal justice the opinions of others; and the hopelessness of establishing a clerical ascendancy would take away from sectarianism the temptation to turbulence and the temporal regard of bigotry. . . . The differences on matters of belief between various classes of Christians would be left open to free discussion and tranquil reasoning. And from contests of that description the Catholic Church would have everything to hope and nothing to fear.[27]

When dying in 1847 O'Connell set out for Rome on the advice of his doctors who hoped that a change of climate might bring recovery. In passing through Paris he received a deputation of Liberal Catholics headed by Montalembert. They had always regarded him as their prototype, and now they presented him with an address which included the passage:

> You then [on Montalembert's visit to Derrynane in 1830] pointed out to us the course we should pursue, and the rules we should follow in order to emancipate the Church from the temporal yoke, by legal and civil means, and at the same time to separate religion from all political causes. Your lessons have fructified amongst us. I am come to present to you the men who in France have enrolled themselves as the first soldiers under a banner you were the first to unfurl. . . . We are all your children or, rather, your pupils; you are our master, our model, our glorious preceptor. It is for that reason we are come to tender you the affectionate and respectful homage we owe to the Man of the age who has done most for the dignity and liberty of mankind and especially for the political instruction of Catholic nations.[28]

O'Connell never reached Rome but died on the way at Genoa, on 15 May 1847. It was a time when the hopes of ihe Liberal Catholics had risen because of the elevation to the Papacy in the previous year of Pius IX. The new pope was apparently a Liberal, and the triumph of Liberalism seemed assured. It was in this atmosphere that two important panegyrics were preached on O'Connell, one in St Peter's in Rome by Ventura, the other in Notre Dame in Paris by Lacordaire. Each pointed to O'Connell's career as a proof of the virtue of Liberal Catholicism and as an encouragement to Liberal Catholics in the future.

Ventura praised O'Connell for having taken the doctrine of liberty of conscience out of the hands of rationalists and proclaimed it throughout Europe; and he expressed the confident hope that Pius IX would walk 'with a firm and sure step in the path that O'Connell had opened' in order to bring about 'the triumph of the Catholic faith and of the Catholic Church by means of liberty.'[29]

In Paris, Lacordaire stressed the consideration that O'Connell had never sought freedom merely for his own religion but for all religions, never merely for his own country but for all countries. Then he exclaimed, 'Catholics, remember that if you desire freedom for yourselves, you must desire it for all mankind. If you demand it only for yourselves it will never be granted to you: give it where you are masters so that you will be given it where you are slaves.'[30]

Many years after his death O'Connell was paid an interesting tribute by the English statesman, Gladstone. Originally a Tory and a staunch up-holder of the Anglican establishment, he had become the leader of the

Liberal Party which was committed to religious equality. As Prime Minister in 1883 he supported a bill designed to admit atheists to parliament with a speech in which he said:

> When I was a very young man, in the second year [1834] of my sitting in parliament . . . I heard a speech from Mr. O'Connell which, although at that time I was bound by party allegiance to receive with misgiving and distrust anything he said, made a deep impression upon me and by which, I think, I have ever since been guided. . . . Mr. O'Connell used these words: 'When I see in this country the law allowing men to dispute the doctrine of the Trinity and the divinity of the Redeemer I really think, if I had no other reason, I should be justified in saying that there is nothing beyond that which should be considered worth quarrelling for or which ought to be made the subject of penal restrictions.'[31]

That O'Connell should have escaped censure by Rome for his unorthodox views is easily explained. He lived in the English-speaking Protestant world where Catholicism had little to lose and much to gain from religious freedom and separation of church and state. Furthermore he was a layman, and Rome was more tolerant of heterodoxy in laity than in clergy. His enormous popularity in Ireland and his normally friendly relations with the Irish clergy were additional reasons why Rome would hesitate to confront him. Unlike the French Liberal Catholics, who imprudently appealed to Gregory XVI for a judgment on their principles. O'Connell avoided theological debate in this context. He was careful to express his views in a political rather than a theological frame. It was no accident that in his speech in 1818 he described his ideas as a 'political' creed, and on another occasion he said 'of theology I know nothing and desire to know nothing' though, for a layman, he was well read in theology. It is significant that the only time he is believed to have provoked Papal hostility (the refusal of the privilege of the portable altar) was shortly after he had used the House of Commons as a platform from which to attack the union of church and state in Spain and to encourage the British Government in its anti-Carlist policy.

A more intriguing question is how did he manage to reconcile these views with the Church's official teaching. To put the question in another form, how could a Child of the Enlightenment be a *religieux*? O'Connell did not answer that question nor did he leave us the evidence on which we could base an answer. He never expressly refuted the official teaching and he never put forward reasons in support of his own views. He merely stated them, and no doubt deliberately, left it at that.

3

The eighteenth-century background

Much has been written on Daniel O'Connell, but no historian has tried to set him against his background in eighteenth-century Ireland. A serious examination has been made of his views on the Gaelic language[2] as he found it in his early years, and some attention, however inadequate, has been paid to the origins of his attitude to violence. But other aspects of his relationship to the Ireland of his youth have scarcely been studied at all. These include his loyalty to the British crown, his veneration for Grattan and 'Grattan's Parliament' his early associations in the legal profession, his attitude to the Irish Protestant Ascendancy and his views on separation of church and state.

I have edited O'Connell's correspondence,[1] which has brought new sources to light and has made it necessary to investigate much old and half-forgotten material. The information obtained has made it appropriate to attempt this study of O'Connell against his environment in eighteenth-century Ireland.

The aspect of O'Connell that is perhaps the most relevant to Ireland today is his espousal of moral force and constitutional methods and his hostility to violence (see Chapter 5).

There is another aspect of O'Connell which historians have neglected to deal with. It is his unequivocal loyalty to the British Crown. Many in the twentieth century have been puzzled by such a loyalty on the part of this quintessential Irishman. They have felt that he must have lacked a full sense of independence or that he was servile in some curious way. There is no great mystery about the matter to anyone versed in Irish history. O'Connell was the product of his age and social background — but historians have not attempted to give any explanation. They have just stated the fact and left it at that. In order to appreciate O'Connell's attitude one must first consider the historical background to the political loyalty of Irish Catholics of the propertied classes towards the end of the eighteenth century.

Through the centuries after the Norman invasion the people of Ireland, whether of the Pale, the Norman-Irish areas or the Gaelic parts of the country, accepted the English kings as lords of Ireland. No doubt that acceptance in some areas was informed by a spirit of loyalty while in others was based on a passive recognition of the status quo. The Reformation and the complete conquest of the whole country by the Tudors introduced new complications, but the bulk of the Catholic population continued to recognize the sovereignty of the English crown. There were rebellions against English rule — that of Hugh O'Neill at the end of the sixteenth century being the most serious — but these never had the support of the majority of Catholic leaders, clerical or lay. Such rebellions, even when enjoying Spanish or Papal support, could scarcely be regarded as 'national movements' in any modern sense.[3]

In the seventeenth century Irish Catholics supported Charles I in the struggle between king and parliament: in the (Catholic) Confederation of Kilkenny they took as their motto, 'Pro Deo et Rege.'[4] At the time of the Glorious Revolution Catholics fought in large numbers in the army of James II and continued to give their loyalty to the exiled Stuarts into the eighteenth century. The Penal Laws, deriving from the sixteenth century though mainly enacted in the late seventeenth and early eighteenth centuries, made it difficult for Irish Catholics to recognize the accession of the Hanoverians to the British throne. Debarred from entry to parliament, government service and the professions, and suffering other serious disabilities, they went abroad to take service in Continental armies.

The position of Catholics was complicated and rendered more vulnerable by the fact that the Papacy continued to acknowledge the Stuarts as the legitimate sovereigns until the death of James III in 1766. This recognition involved allowing the Stuarts the right of nominating to Irish bishoprics. It bore heavily on Catholics, since it laid them open to the charge of political disloyalty and served as an argument in favour of the retention of the Penal Laws. By the death of James III, however, it was clear that all hope of a Stuart restoration to the British throne was gone, and the Papacy refrained from acknowledging the claims of his son, Charles III (Bonnie Prince Charlie). The way now lay open for Irish Catholics to come to terms with the House of Hanover, that is, to give their explicit loyalty to George III and seek relief from the Penal Laws.

Realizing that there could be no hope of having these laws repealed until Catholics formally declared their loyalty to the British sovereign, the Catholic Committee — a body of landowners and merchants of a loosely representative character — were most anxious that the Irish Parliament should pass an act providing an oath of political allegiance which would enable Catholics to qualify as loyal subjects. In 1774 such an oath was enacted but it contained several phrases — most of them implicitly insulting to the Pope — which many Catholics found unpalatable. A number of prominent laymen and some of the bishops took the oath, but other bishops refused and sought a formal condemnation from Rome. Though expressing strong disapproval of the oath Rome refrained from condemning it. For a time the Committee was deeply divided on the matter, but by 1778 virtually all opposition to the oath was abandoned.[5]

Daniel O'Connell's forebears were among the limited number of Gaelic and Catholic landowning families who survived the turmoil and confiscations of the sixteenth and seventeenth centuries and emerged into the late eighteenth century still in possession of some of their ancestral property. It is almost certain that many of O'Connell's relatives took the 1774 oath, as did the bulk of propertied Catholics. His uncle, the head of the family, Maurice (Hunting-Cap) O'Connell, must have done so, since he was made a Justice of the Peace on the passing of the Catholic Relief Act of 1793 (the measure which made it possible for Catholics to hold this appointment), and the taking of the oath would have been a prerequisite for this (unpaid) position. One can take it as certain also that the O'Connells, as members of the Catholic propertied classes, saw no difficulty in recognizing George III as King of Ireland as well as Great Britain. O'Connell's great-grandfather, John O'Connell, and many of his other relatives, had fought in the army of James II. On the passing of the first Catholic relief act, that of 1778, O'Connell's uncle, Lt Col. Daniel Charles O'Connell, showed that he fully recognized the sovereignty of the British Crown over Ireland when he wrote home from France:

> A Revolution so unexpected and so long wished for must needs procure, in course of some years, an accession to the power and prosperity of the Kingdom of Ireland, and unite in one common Sentiment of loyalty the hearts of that long-oppressed and long unfortunate Nation. One step more still remains to be made — I mean the Liberty of spilling their blood in defence of their King and Country. I doubt not 'twill soon be granted tho' no motive cu'd ever induce me to bear arms against France, where I early found an Asylum when refused one at home.[6]

Thus it was perfectly natural for a man of O'Connell's family and social background to recognize the sovereignty over Ireland of the English Crown

But Irishmen in the twentieth century are puzzled not merely because O'Connell recognized the Crown but also because he did it so exuberantly. Again, there is no mystery. Throughout his public life he was constantly accused of being disloyal to the British connection, so that he was obliged to proclaim his loyalty to the Crown frequently and loudly. Then there was the fact that he was committed to leading his people away from lawlessness and into constitutional paths. It would help that purpose considerably if he could awaken in his followers a lively sentiment of veneration for the Crown. His enthusiasm for Queen Victoria, his 'darlin' little Queen', has attracted special attention, some of his biographers attributing it to his sense of chivalry. But there was a more substantial reason for it. In the early years of her reign Victoria was a Whig and thereby, whether she realized it or not, a friend to what Irish historians call the Drummond Administration. O'Connell labelled that administration the best that Ireland had ever known and he was determined to keep it in office. When the Whig Government resigned in 1839 the Queen had to ask the Tory leader, Sir Robert Peel, to form a cabinet. Before taking office Peel insisted that she must replace her Whig Ladies of the Bed-chamber with Tories, thus precipitating what is known in British history as the Bedchamber Crisis. She obstinately rejected his demand, whereupon he declined to form a government, and the Whigs came back to power for a further two years. Meetings in both Britain and Ireland congratulated the Queen for so bravely standing up to a Tory 'despotism,' and one English gathering applauded her for refusing to let 'her Belles be Peeled.' O'Connell's affection owed as much to political considerations as to chivalry.

In appraising his attitude to the political institutions of his time it is vital to remember that he was born into a family that not only had lineage but — and this was more important — had achieved economic success. His uncle, Hunting-Cap, had added enormously to his patrimony by farming, smuggling, lending money, thrift and hard bargaining. By the end of the century he was a rich man. O'Connell's father followed Hunting Cap's example, though on a more modest scale and more humanely. He ran a general store, reared ten children and died prosperous. This combination of lineage and economic success meant that O'Connell grew up without that inferiority complex and consequent envy and bitterness so frequent among Irish Catholics. He could look the British Government and the Irish Protestant Ascendancy straight in the face and not feel it necessary to hate them.

But O'Connell's attitude to the political establishment towards the end of the eighteenth century, to the institution known as 'Grattan's Parliament' went beyond mere loyal acceptance: it was one of enthusiasm. This can best be shown by comparing his outlook with that of Hunting-Cap. The first evidence of this enthusiasm can be found in the alarm created at the end of 1796 by the danger of a French invasion.

This alarm was sounded by the appearance of a French fleet in Bantry Bay on the south-west coast, not far from Derrynane where Hunting-Cap resided, in December 1796. Wolfe Tone, the founder of the United Irishmen, was on board, the project owing much to his persuasive powers with the French Government. But a large part of the fleet had been dispersed by a storm, and when it did not arrive, the ships in Bantry Bay weighed anchor and returned to France. Hunting-Cap was informed of the arrival of the French fleet, and immediately sent word to the authorities in Tralee, the county town of Kerry.

As a law student in Dublin O'Connell shared in the general excitement and was full of eagerness to join one of the lawyers' yeomanry corps. However, as Hunting-Cap's heir, he had first to obtain his uncle's permission. Two of three letters in January, 1797 from the young man to Hunting-Cap on this issue are extant.[7] It appears from this correspondence that O'Connell had earlier been refused permission, but with the news from Bantry Bay he renewed his plea. He pointed out that the present alarm had induced nearly all members of the legal profession in Dublin to take up arms. Should he be the only one not to do so he would come under the unfavorable notice of the Government (a point likely to influence Hunting-Cap). He added that he was 'young, active, healthy and single,' and attributed his eagerness to being 'surrounded as I am with young men whom the moment has inspired with enthusiasm; with the blood of youth boiling in my veins, you will not be surprised that I should be more than usually animated.'

In the second of these letters O'Connell tactfully expressed concern lest he might have pressed his uncle too warmly for the permission, and he attributed his ardour to 'the danger I was in of being looked upon by the men who are to be my companions and fellow labourers through life, as a coward or a scoundrel, or as both.' He ended this letter by giving a more self-interested reason why he was opposed to a French invasion:

> That invasion which if successful should have shook the foundation of all property, would have destroyed our profession root and branch. All that I have read, all that I have thought, all that I have combined was about to be rendered nugatory at once. It was little but this little was my all.

The requested permission was apparently given but obviously with reluctance. In future years Hunting-Cap was to advise his nephew repeatedly to apply himself to his profession and not become too deeply involved in the struggle for Catholic Emancipation. He was no doubt advising him now to concentrate on legal studies rather than indulge in semi-military activities.

It is generally agreed by historians that the bulk of propertied Catholics

in Ireland supported the passing of the Act of Union between Great Britain
and Ireland in 1800, and were encouraged to do so by the virtual promise
that Emancipation would follow. O'Connell was the only member of the
Catholic community[8] who is known to have stood out prominently against
Catholics generally on this issue. He did so by addressing a Catholic
meeting in Dublin in January 1800. It appears from the press reports that
he was the only speaker, and he proposed five anti-Union resolutions
which were adopted unanimously.[9]

In his address he explained that the Catholics of Dublin had earlier
decided to stand aloof, as a sect, from political discussion, but it had now
become necessary for them to come forward, as a sect, to contradict the
false and scandalous charge that 'the Roman Catholics of Ireland were
friends to the measure of Union.' He described the Union as 'the political
murder of our country,' and ended his speech with the words:

> I know that although exclusive advantages may be ambiguously held
> forth to the Irish Catholic to seduce him from the sacred duty which
> he owes his country; I know that the Catholics of Ireland still
> remember that they have a country, and that they will never accept
> of any advantages as a *sect*, which would debase and destroy them
> as a *people*.

This address provoked a stern rebuke from his uncle. In a long letter[10]
Hunting-Cap declared he had for some years disapproved of the 'unwise
and intemperate' conduct of the Catholics, 'whether they assumed the
character of the Catholic Convention or of the aggregate or select meeting
of the Catholics of Dublin.' They seemed to him to have completely lost
sight of the fact that they owed the favours they had received not to the
Irish Parliament but to the British Government, and that it was to that
government that they must look for future favours. This consideration was
all the more important now that 'the Orange Lodges are rapidly spreading
through the Kingdom and that the hostile and rancorous spirit that forms
and pervades them is so generally known.' He regretted to observe that
these Catholics had

> all along been the dupes of designing and insidious men, who under
> a mask of fellowfeeling and liberal friendship were slyly and assidu-
> ously and treacherously urging them on to their ruin, subtly de-
> preciating the favours they received, and artfully holding out objects
> not attainable at the moment, to excite their impatience and involve
> them in ill-timed and intemperate measures and demands.

He ended his strictures with the warning:

> I know you have a facility of disposition which exposes you to rather
> an incautious compliance with those you live in habits of friendship
> with, and I am also aware that professional young men are in general
> disposed to accede to measures that place them in a conspicuous point
> of view. In some instances it may be useful, very frequently not. The
> little temporary attentions it produces soon expire. Popular applause
> is always short-lived but the inconveniences may be serious and
> lasting. In the present case I must earnestly recommend that you keep
> clear of all farther interference, the part you have taken must have
> rendered you unacceptable to Government, and it is therefore
> necessary you should be particularly circumspect and correct with
> respect to your words and conduct.

In this passage Hunting-Cap was no doubt referring to the United
Irishmen, and more definitely, to anti-Union Protestants whom he saw as
exerting an undesirable influence over his nephew.[11]

Hunting-Cap's hostility to the Irish Parliament because of its attitude to
Catholics was not new. In 1780 the Knight of Kerry, one of the M.P.s for
Co. Kerry, asked him if the Catholics of his neighbourhood, Iveragh,
would combine with the Protestants to form a corps of Volunteers (the
voluntary yeomanry of that time).[12] Hunting-Cap rejected the request on
the ground that it was illegal for Catholics to bear arms, and he took the
opportunity to express his very unfavourable opinion of the Irish
Parliament:

> I am fully convinced that the Roman Catholic gentlemen of Iveragh
> would readily unite with their Protestant neighbours to form a corps
> did they think such a measure would meet the approbation of the
> Legislature. They would, in common with every Catholic of standing
> in Ireland, be exceedingly happy by every means in their power to
> give additional weight and strength and security to the kingdom; but
> what can they do while the laws of their country forbid them the use
> of arms? Under such circumstances I look upon it to be their duty to
> confine themselves to that line of conduct marked out for them by
> the Legislature, and with humility and resignation wait for a further
> relaxation of the laws, which a more enlightened and liberal way of
> thinking, added to a clearer and more deliberate attention to the real
> interests and prosperity of the country, will, I hope, soon bring
> about.[13]

O'Connell's opposition to the Union no doubt owed much to the fact that he was a member of the Irish bar. Quite early in the great debate on that measure an indignant meeting of barristers in Dublin condemned the Union by a vote of 166 to 32.[14] But the opposition of the bar could be predicted. Barristers are traditionally associated with law-making as members of parliament and as drafters of legislation. The loss of a legislature would mean a loss of business for the profession and a decline in status since many barristers were in the House of Commons and the chief judges sat in the Lords.

There is an entirely different consideration but one which also arises from the fact that O'Connell was a fledgling barrister in these last years of the eighteenth century. His nearest friends would have been law students and newly qualified barristers, and he was of a gregarious disposition who made friends and acquaintances readily. One can safely assume that fully eighty per cent of his young companions in the legal profession were Protestants,[15] and his association with them would help to explain why he adopted an attitude to the Union very different from that held by the bulk of propertied Catholics. There is the further consideration that he had abandoned the faith in which he was reared and was now a rationalist. This would make it all the easier for him to be influenced by those not Catholic.

At the Dublin Catholic meeting in 1800, which has been described, O'Connell proposed five anti-Union resolutions which included the statements:

> The proposed incorporate Union of the legislatures of Great Britain and Ireland is, in fact, an extinction of the liberty of this country. . . . The improvement of Ireland for the last twenty years, so rapid beyond example, is to be ascribed wholly to the independency of our legislature, so gloriously asserted in the year 1782 by virtue of our parliament cooperating with the generous recommendation of our most gracious and benevolent sovereign and backed by the spirit of our people. If that independency should ever be surrendered, we must as rapidly relapse into our former depression and misery; and . . . Ireland must inevitably lose with her liberty all that she has acquired in wealth and industry and civilization.

Though modern historians would find this evaluation of 'Grattan's Parliament' much too rose-tinted, it remained part of O'Connell's political *dicta* throughout his life. He repeatedly praised that parliament and never ceased to express veneration for Grattan. In 1810, for example, he addressed a Dublin meeting in favour of the repeal of the Act of Union, and ended a long speech with the plea,

Let that spirit which heretofore emanating from Dungannon [the great meeting of the Volunteers in 1782] spread all over the island, and gave light and liberty to the land, be again cherished amongst us. Let us rally round the standard of Old Ireland, and we shall easily procure that greatest of political blessings, an Irish King, an Irish House of Lords, and an Irish House of Commons.[16]

When Grattan died in 1820 O'Connell proposed his son, Henry Grattan, Jr., to be his father's successor as M.P. for Dublin City. He commenced his speech on this occasion with the words:

We are met on this melancholy occasion to celebrate the obsequies of the greatest man Ireland ever knew.... In 1778, when Ireland was shackled, he reared the standard of independence; and in 1782 he stood forward as the champion of his country, achieving gloriously her independence. After the disastrous act of Union, which met his most resolute and most determined opposition, he did not suffer despair to creep over his heart and induce him to abandon her, as was the case with too many others. His life, to the very period of his latest breath, has been spent in her service — and he died, I may even say, a martyr in her cause.[17]

His veneration for Grattan survived the bitterness of the Veto controversy. This issue arose from the proposal in 1813 and subsequent years to procure Catholic Emancipation by granting to the British government a right of veto in the nomination of bishops. Grattan gave the most decided support to this proposal but O'Connell rejected it utterly and treated many of its protagonists to no small amount of invective. But his censure of Grattan was mild, and qualified by praise of his past labours. Probably the harshest comment he ever made on Grattan formed part of a speech on the Veto in 1815:

I see with regret that, except his services in our Cause, he has since the Union made no exertions worthy of his name and of his strength. Since he has inhaled the foul and corrupt atmosphere that fills some of the avenues to Westminster, there have not been the same health and vigour about him.... I feel for him unfeigned respect; but he has refused to accept the Petition [to the House of Commons for Emancipation] upon our terms.[18]

O'Connell's restraint was all the more significant because, in an address to the Catholics of Ireland, Grattan described him as a shallow and cowardly opportunist.[19]

An indication that his veneration for Grattan did not diminish with the years can be seen in an incident that occurred in 1843. In that year the *Dublin Review*, of which O'Connell was a founder, published a review of the *Grattan Memoirs*[20] that amounted to a scurrilous attack on Grattan's public character and reputation. O'Connell must have expressed indignation because the magazine's temporary editor, Revd Nicholas (later Cardinal) Wiseman, wrote him an apologetic explanation of 'some circumstances connected with the article on Grattan in the last number, which I find gave you pain.'[21]

It is of course true that O'Connell had good reason to remain on friendly terms with Grattan. The old man had done his life's work, but he was a revered figure in the British Parliament and enjoyed the respect of a great many Irishmen, Protestant and Catholic. He could still be a useful ally. It was good politics to try to quiet Protestant fears by portraying the Repeal of the Act of Union as merely a return to a happy constitutional position rather than a leap into the future. Nevertheless, O'Connell's praise of Grattan and 'Grattan's Parliament' went far beyond what was necessary for these aims, and was clearly inspired by a positive enthusiasm. That sentiment was not shared by Hunting-Cap, whose disdain for the Irish Parliament has been shown, nor by the bulk of propertied Catholics, since they supported the Union which involved the destruction of that late eighteenth-century constitution.

O'Connell saw the historic Irish nation as the Catholic population in existence before the Reformation. Paradoxically, he regarded Grattan and the Protestant Ascendancy as Irish, and their Parliament, even though it excluded Catholics, as a great and traditional Irish institution. In neither speech nor writing did he ever suggest that they were *colons* or that their parliament was a colonial institution. It is true that later generations of Irish Catholic nationalists came to see the Protestant Ascendancy and the eighteenth-century parliament as colonial, but that development owed more to Thomas Davis[22] and Romantic nationalism than to O'Connell. Though a Protestant, Davis was hostile to the landlord classes who were the backbone of that ascendancy. In many articles in *The Nation* he denounced the landlords as tyrannical, anti-Irish and alien in race and religion to the people of Ireland. He was scarcely conscious of the extent to which these widely read articles were identifying the nation with Catholicism and cutting off the Protestants. By a curious contradiction he also claimed that the nation comprised men of all religions and of different racial stocks — Gael, Norman and English. It was only the landlords he denounced as alien, but a later generation could find it easy to conclude that if landlord Protestants were alien in race and religion then all Protestants must be alien. The struggle over the land and Home Rule encouraged Catholics to pay more attention to Davis's denunciation of Irish landlords as alien than to his more modestly expressed definition of an Irish nation as inclusive of all religious and racial stocks.

In order to understand how O'Connell could identify with both the historic nation, which he saw as Catholic, and the eighteenth-century nation, whose constitutional leadership was exclusively Protestant, one must remember that he was a child of the Enlightenment. A rationalist in early manhood and having the utilitarian and universal outlook of the Enlightenment he had no difficulty in seeing the whole community as the nation. It was Romanticism which encouraged an interest in racial origins and traditions, a potentially disruptive development in Ireland where religious difference marked off the Protestants, mostly descended from seventeenth-century immigrants, from the older, Catholic, stocks.[23] Furthermore, Romanticism gave to nationalism a sacredness and vigour which quickly led to intransigence. Where O'Connell saw self-government as vital to good government, the Young Irelanders saw self-government as an end in itself, a spiritual necessity. Thus support for Repeal became an essential part of Irish nationality, a way of separating nationalist from alien. By the mid-1840s O'Connell's old-fashioned all-inclusive eighteenth-century nationalism was giving way to the new Romantic nationalism which would exclude those — in effect, the Protestants — refusing to support Repeal.

Finally one must point to another sphere — relations between church and state — in which O'Connell must have been deeply influenced by the experience of eighteenth-century Ireland. This subject is discussed in Chapter 2.

O'Connell emerges from this study a man more closely tied to his eighteenth-century environment than historians have usually thought. His espousal of the cause of separation of church and state undoubtedly owed much to the unhappy effects of the continued Papal recognition of the exiled Stuarts and also to the surprising amount of freedom from state interference in its internal ecclesiastical structure which the Catholic Church enjoyed in eighteenth-century Ireland. His adoption of constitutional methods and his aversion to violence can be ascribed much more to his Irish experience than to his sojourn in revolutionary France. O'Connell's loyalty to the British crown, which has puzzled much Irish popular and even educated opinion, was natural and reasonable for a man of his religious and political traditions. He accepted the political institutions of late eighteenth-century Ireland, including the exclusively Protestant Parliament, as Irish; and he accepted them with a certain enthusiasm. It seems clear that this enthusiasm owed much to the influence exerted on him as a young man by his Protestant colleagues at the Irish bar. Seeking justice and equality for Catholics and attempting to obtain the repeal of the Act of Union he had to spend most of his public life attacking the Protestant Ascendancy, yet he always regarded its members as Irishmen. In this he differed from later generations of Catholic nationalists who frequently tended to see those Protestants, and indeed all Irish Protestants, as alien.

4

Collapse and recovery

Change in the interpretation of the past is an important part of history. The changing evaluation of historical ideas, movements and persons is also of considerable interest, not only to professional historians but to a much wider circle. It is perhaps that part of history which is the most useful to leaders in society since it is probably the only part which yields some indication of what the course of affairs is likely to be in the foreseeable future, of the way 'things are going'. For Irishmen the present is so consciously linked to the past that this study of change is of special interest and value. In modern Irish history and even in present Irish politics Daniel O'Connell is a controversial figure: praise of him can provoke irritation. Consequently the vicissitudes of his reputation over the past century make a relevant and worthwhile study.

In the generation after his death O'Connell was regarded as the Moses who had led a Catholic people out of bondage. He was seen as the defender of his people in the law courts, the champion who won Catholic Emancipation and organized the Repeal movement, the protagonist of religious freedom for Irish Catholics against the British Government and the Irish Protestant Ascendancy. A discordant note was struck by some of the Young Irelanders, notably John Mitchel, in their publications in the fifteen years after O'Connell's death, but his popularity was too strong to be seriously affected by these attacks. More important in this context were the disestablishment of the Church of Ireland and the Land Acts of the 1880s. These measures virtually completed the rout of the Protestant Ascendancy and thereafter the memory of the Catholic defender was no longer needed.

Just at this time, the early 1880s, Charles Gavan Duffy produced his two most effective historical works — *Young Ireland* and *Four Years of Irish History 1845-1849*. These semi-autobiographical books dealt with the differences which had led to a bitter quarrel between O'Connell and the Young Irelanders. In order to justify the young men, of whom he himself had been one, Duffy portrayed O'Connell as a great political leader whose character was marred by greed and intolerance and by a lack of integrity. Appearing some forty years after O'Connell's death, and just when his memory was no longer needed, Duffy's writings dealt hammer blows at O'Connell's reputation. Mitchel's charge that O'Connell's doctrine of moral force rendered the people helpless during the Famine — a thesis that could be induced from much that Duffy wrote — now found acceptance.

Irish nationalist opinion was now ready to adopt policies based on the violence that was being widely preached throughout Europe towards the end of the nineteenth century and into the middle of the twentieth century. The success of Sinn Féin as against the failure of the Home Rule Party converted a majority of the Catholic population to a new confidence in violence. It was not long before O'Connell, the man of moral force and constitutional methods, was seen as an effete politician.

In the generation that followed Duffy's publications O'Connell's biographers were Michael MacDonagh (1903) and Denis Gwynn (1929). They both dealt very briefly with O'Connell's last years, obviously feeling as admirers of his that the less said about his quarrel with the Young Irelanders the better.

The rot was stopped at the intellectual, though not at the popular, level, by the appearance in 1938 of Seán Ó Faoláin's brilliant study of O'Connell's personality, *King of the Beggars*. Artist rather than professional historian, Ó Faoláin portrayed O'Connell as a complex and interesting man, the founder of Irish democracy, and the greatest political leader in modern Ireland. This interpretation reflected the author's disenchantment with the Sinn Féin Revolution.

O'Connell's reputation reached its nadir in popular opinion in the 1940s. At the Davis Centenary Celebrations in Trinity College, Dublin, in 1945 the President of Ireland, the late Sean T. O'Kelly, compared in his address the eloquence of Davis with the *plámas* of O'Connell.[1] In 1947 the Abbey Theatre put on *The Great Pacificator*, a play of little dramatic merit which expressed Duffy's interpretation of the O'Connell-Young Ireland quarrel and Mitchel's charge concerning non-violence and the Famine. In the following year the final blow was delivered by a South Kerry amateur dramatic society in staging this play. In 1947 the Dublin-based but largely Kerry body, the Save Derrynane Committee, issued an appeal for funds to have O'Connell's home preserved as a national monument, It was symptomatic of his fall from political grace that the Committee found it expedient to ground its propaganda on the Catholic leader rather than the political leader. A member of the Committee told the present writer that the appeal for funds would have a much better chance of success had O'Connell died after winning Emancipation.[2]

In 1947 R. Dudley Edwards, Professor of Modern Irish History in University College Dublin, said that it would take thirty years of historical writing to restore O'Connell to his true place in Irish history. It seemed a rash prophecy but time has proved it sound. The beginning of the restoration at the level of professional history came in 1947 with Denis Gwynn's 'O'Connell, Davis and the Colleges Bill' in the *Irish Ecclesiastical Record* (it was later published as a book). In this work Gwynn virtually redrafted Duffy's account of the differences between O'Connell and Davis in 1844-45 in a way which pointed to Davis as excitable and provocative and to O'Connell as patient and reasonable. The year 1949 saw the publication of *Daniel O'Connell: Nine Centenary Essays*. Its editor was Michael Tierney, a classical scholar and President of University College Dublm. His aim, as stated in the foreword, was to rescue O'Connell's memory from the disrepute into which it had fallen and to 'present his character and his work in a more objective and more truly historical light'. Owing to the sparsity of Irish historical scholarship at the time, Tierney had to cast his net wide for contributors. Though the book contained its share of nuggets it seems to have made only a limited impact on academic opinion.

In 1956 *The Great Famine*,[3] particularly Thomas P. O'Neill's article on famine relief schemes, provided a new interpretation and showed by implication that the Famine's disastrous effect on the people could not reasonably be blamed on O'Connell's policy of non-violence. In 1963 Professor Kevin Nowlan produced a little read but important monograph, *Charles Gavan Duffy and the Repeal Movement*. In this he buttressed Denis Gwynn's adverse criticism of the Young Irelanders and drew several conclusions favourable to O'Connell. But *The Politics of Repeal* in 1965 by the same author, though an able description of the 1840s, was too cautious in its treatment of O'Connell and Young Ireland to have much influence on contemporary thinking in that context.

The year 1965 saw the publication of Dr Angus Macintyre's *The Liberator: Daniel O'Connell and the Irish Party 1830-1847*. This book contains a mass of detailed but relevant information on the activities and policies of O'Connell as a parliamentary leader. Of its very nature such a book is not for the general reader, but it brings home to the historian a sense of O'Connell's amazing political energy and ingenuity. The later 1960s brought three more general works, James C. Beckett's *The Making of Modern Ireland 1603-1923*, Lawrence J. McCaffrey's *The Irish Question 1800-1922* and Oliver MacDonagh's *Ireland*. These books praised O'Connell highly, and since they were not admiring biographies, the praise was more valuable than that of Michael MacDonagh and Denis Gwynn. Since Beckett is an Irish Protestant his evaluation of O'Connell may be compared with that of Lecky in his *Leaders of Public Opinion in*

Ireland a century previously. Lecky wrote:

> The more I dwell upon the subject the more I am convinced of the splendour and originality of the genius and of the reality of the patriotism of O'Connell, in spite of the animosities that surround his memory and the many grievous faults that obscured his life.

Beckett writes:

> O'Connell's great contribution to the development of modern Ireland was that he called into being, and organised for political action, the force of mass opinion; he taught the Roman Catholic majority to regard itself as the Irish nation; and all succeeding nationalist leaders . . . have had to build on the foundations that he laid. . . . But when all this [concerning his defects] has been said, he remains a man of transcendent genius, which he devoted to the service of his native land: no other single person has left such an unmistakable mark on the history of Ireland.

Since these two appraisals are separated by a hundred years the substantial similarity between them is striking. O'Connell emerges from the pages of both historians a great political leader and a great man. The wheel has come full cycle.

The year 1972 saw the publication of Robert Kee's *The Green Flag: a History of Irish Nationalism* and Gearóid Ó Tuathaigh's *Ireland before the Famine 1798-1848*. Kee points to several instances in which historians have been misled by Duffy in regard to O'Connell; and Ó Tuathaigh praises the Young Irelanders but censures them for political immaturity and for their 'holier-than-thou' attitude to O'Connell.

The spring of 1975 heard a series of eight Thomas Davis Lectures on O'Connell from Radio Telefís Éireaun. The authors were: Joseph Lee, Angus Macintyre, Donal McCartney, John A. Murphy, Kevin B. Nowlan (the editor of the series), Maurice R. O'Connell, Diarmuid Ó Muirithe and T. Desmond Williams. I forbear to comment on my own contribution but can say that each of the other seven was written by an authority in his field and made a serious contribution to knowledge of O'Connell, and most of them were of high calibre. The very fact that scholars could find enough in O'Connell for eight lectures on different topics — there was no overlapping, and several aspects of the man were left untouched —is a proof in itself of his return to favour in academic opinion.

I have paid much attention to O'Connell's quarrel with the Young Irelanders, or to be more precise, to their interpretation of that quarrel. It was that interpretation which paved the way for the destruction of his stature in the eyes of Irishmen in the twentieth century. Since 1945 no historian has attempted to justify the Young Irelanders, while nearly every historian has found something commendable in O'Connell.

The editing of O'Connell's correspondence,[4] which I undertook in 1967, has brought to light a mass of new information. It provides a fresh and much more comprehensive understanding of O'Connell's private life, particularly his relations with his wife, a much more interesting woman than had formerly been thought, and with his children. It tells us much more about his life as a lawyer and as a landlord. It informs us of one major facet of his life that had only been suspected — his extravagance with money, a source of constant tension between himself and his wife.[5]

The charge that O'Connell was sexually promiscuous has always provoked controversy. The correspondence indicates that he sowed wild oats as a young man before his marriage but that is not really the charge which is, rather, one of sustained adultery. Professor Helen Mulvey of Connecticut College has examined all the letters extant between O'Connell and his wife (660 of his and 240 of hers), and she concludes:

> On the subject of O'Connell's marital fidelity, on the accusations of Ellen Courtenay and the later statements of Sir James O'Connor and W. B. Yeats, the letters have nothing explicit to say. But the substance and tone of the correspondence as a whole are powerful evidence of O'Connell's fidelity and devotion to his wife and of his deep happiness in every aspect of his relationship with her.[6]

No reliable evidence has ever been provided to support the belief that O'Connell was promiscuous, but any statement to this effect is immediately met by the popular rejoinder: 'But everybody knows he was'. The solution to the mystery has been provided by the folklorists.[7] O'Connell is the principal folk-hero in modern Irish history, and in Irish folklore sexual prowess is always attributed to the hero. In a recent public lecture Dr Diarmuid Ó Muirithe of University College Dublin says of O'Connell:

> All over the country the people told stories about his fabulous virility. Rathkeale in County Limerick stands indicted as the only town in Ireland that didn't provide a woman for his bed: his mistresses were legion and they included Queen Victoria!

All these stories were a product of the folk-mind. The heroes of old were ever famous for their sexual energy.[8]

This combination of history, correspondence and folklore leads to the (disappointing!) conclusion that O'Connell was a faithful husband.

The letters provide a much more comprehensive knowledge of O'Connell's activities in Britain and his relations with British Whigs and Radicals, his interest in India, anti-slavery, franchise reform, law reform, Chartists, trade unions, and the repeal of the Corn Laws. The charge that O'Connell was 'anti-labour' has been current since the appearance of James Connolly's *Labour in Irish History*. In 1970 Dr Fergus D'Arcy of University College Dublin produced on article[9] on O'Connell's relations with Dublin artisans during the 1830s. He maintains that O'Connell was hostile to certain trade union practices but not necessarily to the unions themselves, and he makes the point that his opposition to these practices was open and courageous. D'Arcy concludes however that O'Connell's economic outlook, if implemented, would have been very damaging to the interests of the town workers. Professor Joseph Lee of University College, Cork, is more sympathetic to O'Connell. In his lecture in 1975[10] he states that O'Connell felt a real concern for the workers but was opposed to certain practices of the organized artisans. He thinks that O'Connell had some cause for this hostility since these Dublin trade unions were limited to the skilled and were 'islands of privilege in a sea of working class poverty', and he adds: 'Once Dublin unionists abandoned violence after 1838, partly as a response to O'Connell's denunciations, he did not again attack them'. Lee warns that O'Connell's attitude to labour must not be confused with that of a *laissez-faire* capitalist employer. His principal criticism of O'Connell is that his *laissez-faire* Liberal approach to economic progress was inadequate for a land materially poor and experiencing a population explosion. Drastic policies involving government intervention were necessary. In his *Ireland* Professor Oliver MacDonagh has made essentially the same point.

O'Connell's attitude to the Gaelic language was the subject of his lecture in 1975 by Professor John A. Murphy of University College, Cork. In an imaginative study which reflects the great strides in Gaelic scholarship in recent years Murphy sees O'Connell as a 'Gaeltacht man' and therefore pragmatic, utilitarian, resourceful, adaptable and 'entirely without sentimentality' about the Gaelic language and way of life. A mastery of the English language was necessary if the people were to survive and advance themselves in a hostile world. His Gaelic background, Murphy continues, his own individual pragmatic temperament, and the fact that he was deeply influenced by the Enlightenment with its concern for the universal at the expense of the local and particular, encouraged him to leave the language to its fate. Even when aware of his views in this context the Gaelic poets of his day were his fervent admirers. Murphy ends his study with the statement:

Later generations which saw the loss of the Irish language and its distinctive culture as calamitous, looked for convenient Anglicising agents and readily found them in Maynooth, the National Schools and Daniel O'Connell, the last being the chief scapegoat. Whether his attitude made much difference to a doomed language, in view of what we now know of the complex phenomena of linguistic change, is extremely problematical. But what is certain is that for his own people he was the last hero of the Gaelic world.[11.]

A subject which has been curiously neglected is O'Connell's attitude to religious freedom. Mr Kennedy F. Roche[12] has touched on this, and Professor Kevin Nowlan in several of his works has insisted that O'Connell's Liberalism was genuine and significant, but no one has dealt with the subject directly. I have attempted to make good this deficiency, though only to a limited extent, by presenting a series of statements by O'Connell with some indication of the background against which they were made.[13] O'Connell was the first Catholic statesman, and perhaps the first in any major Christian denomination in Europe, to espouse both religious freedom and separation of church and state. He was followed some years later by the French Liberal Catholics and by the Italian priest, Gioacchino Ventura, all of whom regarded O'Connell as their prototype. Some Catholic churchmen in Austria at the time of Joseph II favoured religious freedom and equality but subject to a system of state regulation which O'Connell would have found wholly unacceptable. In 1787, 1789 and 1790 Charles James Fox, who was of course an Anglican, committed himself to the cause of religious freedom in speeches in the British House of Commons, but he made it clear that he was not giving any countenance to separation of church and state. Many Europeans in the eighteenth century had expressed approval of religious freedom but their views were coloured by indifference or hostility to religion itself or at least to one or other of the Christian churches. The special importance of O'Connell and the Continental Liberal Catholics in this context lay in the fact that they were practising Catholics.

The generation after his death venerated O'Connell as the great defender of religious freedom but left in the air the question whether his concern was limited to the interests of Irish Catholics or extended to all religious bodies. It is now seen clearly that he was concerned with religious freedom and separation of church and state not only for Ireland but for all countries, including France, Spain and even the Papal States.

Today the most energetic charge against O'Connell is that his opposition to the Colleges bill in 1845 was incompatible with his stand on religious freedom. The charge is incorrectly drawn. O'Connell was concerned with relations between religious denominations and between religious denominations and the state. How a religious body arranges for the education of its members, whether along denominational or inter-denominational lines, is not in any direct way concerned with religious freedom. The charge, correctly stated, is that he helped to perpetuate hostility between Catholics and Protestants by opposing inter-denominational education — the situation in Northern Ireland being seen as, in part, the end-product of that policy. The charge has a certain validity but the divisive effects of denominational education must not be exaggerated — in this context they usually are — and its benefit in terms of moral training must not be ignored.

At the academic level O'Connell's reputation has been restored. He is now respected as a man of a certain universal significance and as a great Irishman, and most historians consider him the greatest political leader of modern Ireland. This respect rests on a sounder and wider base than the adulation paid him by the generation following his death. Popular acceptance of this academic appraisal lags behind but is growing in strength. Romantic nationalism, the confidence in the efficacy of violence, the attribution of great wisdom to 1916, and the belief that the Sinn Féin Revolution of 1919-1921 was an overwhelming success, have been in retreat for some time. The Northern Ireland crisis is the catalyst that is turning that retreat into a rout. Needless to say, historical reputations are never static: the pendulum continues to swing. There seems no doubt that O'Connell will enjoy this high position for a generation. Then what? All one can safely predict is that he is unlikely ever again to fall to the low level that he reached in the first half of the twentieth century.

5

O'Connell, Young Ireland and violence

The volume of the *New Cambridge Modern History* that dealt with the period 1898-1945 was called *The Era of Violence*. With the extension rather than the diminution of brutality and passionate hostility since 1945 it now looks as if limiting that title to the first half of this century has been a mistake. Physical brutality and the regimentation of men's minds have reached such a level of persevering intensity that the twentieth century may yet qualify as the most violent hundred years of the past millennium.

Western civilization has been surprised and even shocked by events in Northern Ireland in the 1970s. Though the violence there cannot be compared with the more extensive savagery in many other places, the continuance of brutality there has caused widespread dismay. It has embarrassed Christians of all denominations in the English-speaking world.

Violence in Ireland is not new, and to many historians it is not something unexpected. For the greater part of two centuries that country has witnessed a conflict between two traditions — moral and physical force, constitutionalism and violence. This conflict found its most deliberate and most eloquent expression in 1846, in the debate leading to a bitter quarrel between Daniel O'Connell and the group known as the Young Irelanders. In view of the relevance of this issue to the world today, and not merely to the present struggle in Northern Ireland, the quarrel of 1846 needs to be studied anew.

In order to understand that quarrel one must consider the political background to the Ireland of the eighteen-forties. The country was then part of the United Kingdom, and the Irish administration in Dublin Castle was controlled by the British Government. The Act of Union of 1800 had abolished the exclusively Protestant Irish parliament but preserved the Anglican Protestants as a ruling caste and accorded the Presbyterians a second-class citizenship while perpetuating the Catholics as a subject population.

The first inroad into the British and Anglican control of Ireland was the Catholic Emancipation Act of 1829, though the early practical consequences of this great statute were slight. A narrow franchise, even after the Great Reform Act of 1832, made it difficult to procure the election to parliament of more than a minority of Catholics and 'pro-Catholic' Protestants. In Britain the Tories were determined, and the more conservative Whigs were inclined, to continue to exclude Catholics from the government of Ireland. However, the British Radicals and the more liberal Whigs thought otherwise: they favoured conciliating the Catholics and were ready to come to terms with the Catholic leader, Daniel O'Connell. The opportunity came in the spring of 1835 when a Liberal-Whig Government found itself with only a slight majority over the Tories and in need of the support of O'Connell's Irish Repeal Party of some 30 MP's (of whom more than a third were Protestants). In an arrangement known as the Lichfield House Compact these Whigs (just before taking office) agreed to enact certain measures and to reform the administration of Ireland along lines beneficial to Catholics. In return O'Connell undertook to support their Government and to postpone indefinitely his campaign for the repeal of the Act of Union. In Ireland this arrangement was soon known as the Whig Alliance. It lasted until the return to power of the Tories under Peel in 1841. The first fruits of the Whig Alliance were the appointment to the Irish Government of three distinguished men — the Earl of Mulgrave as Lord-Lieutenant, Viscount Morpeth as Chief Secretary, and Thomas Drummond as Under-Secretary. These three broke the Protestant monopoly of power by destroying the political predominance of the Orange Order and by appointing Catholics to the judiciary, to the higher ranks of a reformed police, and to the public service in general. However, attempts to enact legislative reforms were only partly successful because of the veto power of the overwhelmingly Tory House of Lords who were determined to uphold Anglican ascendancy.

When it had become clear by 1840 that the Whigs were nearing the end of their tenure of office O'Connell returned to his life-long desire to repeal the Act of Union by founding the Loyal National Repeal Association. While the Whigs were still in government he kept this new organization only partially active, but after the return to office of the Tories, and after he had served his year as Lord Mayor of Dublin, he threw himself into the Repeal campaign. He was aided by a group of young men of literary ability and intellectual tastes, soon to be known as the Young Irelanders. In October 1842 they founded a weekly review, *The Nation*, which quickly won a national reputation. This paper preached the new Romantic Nationalism then sweeping through Europe, an ideology opposed to the old eighteenth-century utilitarian nationalism of O'Connell.

The Repeal campaign reached a crescendo in the summer and autumn of 1843 but then experienced a major though not final defeat when it was firmly resisted by Sir Robert Peel's Tory Government which in this stand had the support of the whole body of British Whigs and Radicals. Too intelligent to think that Repeal could be defeated by negative means alone, Peel enacted three measures designed to conciliate the Catholics and wean them away from supporting O'Connell. One of these, the Colleges Bill, led to a serious division between the Young Irelanders, who favoured interdenominational university education, and O'Connell, who opposed it. The bill was enacted, but the hostilities it evoked had not subsided when politics took a new turn in the autumn of 1845 with the announcement that Peel intended to repeal the Corn Laws.

Because of this new development Peel resigned in December 1845 and Lord John Russell tried but failed to form a government. Consequently Peel returned to office, but the unity of the Tory Party, already imperilled by the Maynooth Act six months previously, was shattered. The Protectionist Tories — the majority of the party — were determined to oust Peel at the first opportunity, while the Whigs were only prepared to leave him in office until he had effected the repeal of the Corn Laws.

The situation opened up exciting prospects for O'Connell. His life-long enemies, the Tories, were now split down the middle in a quarrel that involved both principles and personalities; and the Whigs were sure to return to power. In these circumstances a renewal of the Whig Alliance might bring major benefits to the Irish Repeal Party, greater than any in the past. We must now leave this introductory account of the political situation to the end of 1845 and turn to other matters.

The interpretation this study has arrived at differs from that of virtually all other historians.[1] They see O'Connell as the elderly politician whose leadership was being challenged by the Young Irelanders. Earnest and idealistic, and impatient of his manoeuvres and compromises, the young men chafed at the restraints the old leader imposed on them. When O'Connell wished to renew his former alliance with the Whigs in 1846 he was confronted by the Young Irelanders' determined opposition. In order to renew the alliance and to maintain his leadership — this consensus interpretation runs — O'Connell had to oust the young men from the Repeal Association. He deliberately staged a debate on a theoretical issue — the Peace Resolutions — not to serve the cause of moral force, which was not in danger, but merely to expel the Young Irelanders. An opposing interpretation is possible. It maintains that the principle of moral force was in danger, and that O'Connell introduced the Peace Resolutions for the primary purpose of safeguarding that principle. In examining this subject it might be best to start by considering O'Connell's attitude to violence.

Before doing so, however, one can state without fear of contradiction that he was not a pacifist: he accepted the morality of the just war and the necessity for professional armies. The violence he abhorred was of two kinds. One was the revolutionary kind, in uprisings against established government; the other was violence against the community, as in agrarian secret societies, and outrages. He revered the rule of law and condemned all breaking of the law.

This outlook accorded with medieval Christian beliefs on the right of government to demand obedience and on the justification of rebellion only when a government had abused its authority. But O'Connell went further in laying special stress on the evil consequences of rebellion which he saw as only a last resort to remedy a desperate situation. The rebel must be careful to count the cost of his action in blood and damage to the structure of the community. This distrust of rebellion, this pessimism, undoubtedly arose from what O'Connell had seen of the Irish situation in his own day. With its traditional divisions and enmities, religious, racial and economic, and its recent rapid increase of population without a corresponding increase in employment and food supply, together with its deeply felt grievances, Ireland was a land of tinder. An outbreak of political or agrarian violence could lead to chaos. Furthermore, any rebellion must be fought against the wealth and power of a British government determined to maintain its military control of Ireland. Fear of the almost certain consequences of violence as well as hatred of violence itself induced O'Connell to call on his people to obey the law even when that law was unjust. Historians agree that he opposed violence, but they have not grasped how deep his convictions really were. It is therefore necessary to go into some detail.

The first recorded statement of his concern with violence is an entry in his diary for December 1796. In the previous week a French fleet had arrived in Bantry Bay on the south-west coast, though it was to sail away without effecting a landing. The alarm it raised led O'Connell, then a law student in Dublin, to commit himself to paper:

> Liberty is in my bosom less a principle than a passion; but I know that the victories of the French would be attended with bad consequences. The Irish are not yet sufficiently enlightened to bear the Sun of Freedom. Freedom would soon dwindle into licentiousness, they would rob, they would murder. The altar of liberty totters when it is cemented only with blood, when it is supported only with carcasses.[2]

Shortly after the brutal suppression of the Rebellion he wrote:

I dined to-day with Bennett [a Protestant barrister from Co. Wexford], we talked much of the late unhappy rebellion. A great deal of innocent blood was shed. Good God, what a brute man becomes when ignorant and oppressed. O Liberty, what horrors are perpetrated in thy name! May every virtuous revolutionist remember the horrors of Wexford.[3]

In a letter to his wife in 1803 O'Connell commented on Robert Emmet's rebellion: 'A man who could coolly prepare so much bloodshed, so many murders, and such horrors of every kind has ceased to be an object of compassion.'[4] His delight at revolutionary change effected without violence he expressed in a letter to his wife in 1820:

Oh, darling, were you not delighted with the Portuguese revolution? ... What is most consolatory is that all these changes are taking place without bloodshed. Not one human life sacrificed, no plunder, no confiscation, nothing but what every honest man must approve of.[5]

In an 'Address to the People' in 1813 he called on the Catholic population to abandon recourse to secret societies since membership makes them vulnerable to criminal prosecutions and harsh punishments, and he added:

Reflect also upon the inutility of these associations. What utility — what advantage of any description has ever been derived from them? None — none whatsoever! No redress has ever been obtained by their means. They have been quite useless! Nay, worse, they have always produced crimes! — robbery, outrage, murder![6]

He was just as much opposed to agrarian violence as to political. He made no moral distinction between the two. One example of the active steps he took against the agrarian kind is afforded by his letter in 1815 to his friend Owen O'Conor (later O'Conor Don) of Co. Roscommon. Having informed O'Conor that two organizers of the Ribbonmen had recently gone to the Roscommon area he said:

I am sure you will use every exertion to prevent the poor people from being duped by those or any other combinators. It would be the destruction of our cause [Catholic Emancipation] and their own ruin.[7]

The most revealing event in O'Connell's career concerning violence, apart from the Peace Resolutions of 1846, arose from the Doneraile Conspiracy trials in 1829. As their defence counsel he saved the lives of some twenty men charged with conspiracy to murder landlords and magistrates. In conducting their defence he showed that the Crown had resorted to unscrupulous methods in trying to obtain convictions. The London *Times* saw the use of these methods as an indictment of the Irish Administration and demanded reform:

> The administration of the laws must be taken away from one faction, that the other faction may not be justified in considering the law as an instrument in the hands of its enemies.[8]

The trials were a political as well as a legal victory for O'Connell over the Government, a government that was deeply hostile to him. Yet he did not press his advantage. Instead, he made a public statement at the end of the trials which could only blunt the edge of his victory and relieve the Government of much of its embarrassment. He said that the trials

> taught two important lessons which he would have all that heard him to meditate on and appreciate; it first told the guilty . . . that crime is not safe; that a confederacy of guilt is likely to be broken in upon [and the guilty would be punished]. [The second lesson taught was] that the People should always have confidence in the Laws of the Country.[9]

Clearly, he did not relish winning a great courtroom victory when his success could only enhance the prestige of agrarian violence and hinder acceptance of the rule of law.[10] The trials were an example of the problem that was central to his public life: how to combat the tendency to violence and to engender respect for law when confronted by British governments and Irish administrations who frequently enacted and applied the law to keep the Catholics in subjection.[11]

It is often thought that O'Connell violated his own principles in supporting the Latin-American revolt against Spain. In 1820 he sent his son to serve in the army of Bolivar and wrote a letter praising Bolivar as the liberator of his country. O'Connell could plead, as an extenuating circumstance, that the South American situation was not one of simple rebellion: during the Napoleonic Wars (modern) Venezuela and Colombia had won partial independence from Spain, but with the fall of Napoleon the forces of the restored Spanish king, Ferdinand VII, reconquered these territories. Furthermore, Ferdinand had destroyed the attempt to establish representative government in Spain, and he had restored the Inquisition and the union between church and state which O'Connell was later to describe as 'that disastrous connection between church and state which for nearly two centuries has plunged Spain into the deepest moral degradation.'[12] A man of O'Connell's sympathies could see Bolivar as struggling against the re-establishment of religious intolerance and political despotism, and not as a rebel against authority.

It only remains to point out that O'Connell had strong positive reasons for condemning violence and applauding the rule of law. The chief aim of his public life was to raise his people from subjection and to create a democracy. He believed that democracy had its prerequisites — political education, constitutional organizations, repeated exercises of electoral machinery, and reverence for the rule of law. He saw violence as the enemy of this nascent democracy.

It was consistent with those principles that he should have established the Repeal Association on its basis of moral force and non-violence when he founded it in April 1840. Its constitution rested on three principles of which two were

> The total disclaimer of and the total absence from all physical force, violence, or breaches of the law.

and

> The only means to be used are those of peaceful, legal, and constitutional combinations of all classes, sects, and persuasions of her Majesty's loyal subjects, and by the power of public opinion concentrated upon most salutary and always legal means and objects.[13]

The week after it was formally established the Association adopted an address to the Irish nation which substantially included these passages.[14] In a public statement in October 1840, in protest against an anti-Repeal speech made by the Lord Lieutenant, the Association made the assertion that

> We are firmly determined to use no other than legal and constitutional means to effect the Repeal. . . . We are convinced that nothing but the breaking of the law by the advocates of Repeal can ever prevent the glorious accomplishment of that glorious measure.[15]

In November 1843 the Association adopted an address to the people of Ireland signed by O'Connell. It included the passage:

> The principle of my political life, and that in which I have instructed the people of Ireland is, that all ameliorations and improvements in political institutions can be obtained by persevering in a perfectly

peaceable and legal course, and cannot be obtained by forcible means, or if they could be got by forcible means, such means create more evils than they cure, and leave the country worse than they found it.[16]

In September 1844 the Association adopted a set of instructions to its wardens which contained the declaration:

The Loyal National Repeal Association disclaims all force and violence. It proclaims that the cause is to succeed by peace and perseverance, and that the man that violates the law gives strength to the enemies of Ireland.[17]

In January 1846 the Association unanimously passed a resolution which carried the statement that

We will unremittingly persevere in all legal, constitutional, and, above all, all peaceful means, and no other, until we attain the restoration of the legislative independence of Ireland.[18]

This repetition of declarations written into the constitution of the Repeal Association and adopted at various stages in its history must be borne in mind in order to understand the events of 1846. Historians (with the possible exception of P. S. O'Hegarty) have treated the Peace Resolutions of 1846 as something novel. In fact there was no novelty about them: they were merely a vigorous presentation of declarations made repeatedly in the past.

Before ending this description of O'Connell's attitude to violence it is necessary to deal with his use of the threat of violence as opposed to violence itself. Twice in his career he organized great numbers of people and stirred their passions. The first occasion was in the period 1824-29 when he confronted the British Government with the Catholic Association; the second, in 1843, when he addressed a series of monster meetings designed to overawe the British resistance to Repeal. Both were essays in what today we call brinkmanship. In rousing these passions, however, he repeatedly and consistently condemned violence, and he took every precaution to ensure that his followers and the political organizations he formed kept within the law. He took calculated risks, but in the knowledge, justified by the event, that he had the ability to keep the movements he created from erupting into violence. His case against the Young Irelanders was not that they were men of blood but that they were invoking a martial ardour which they would be unable to contain, and that in doing so they were endangering the belief in and practice of constitutional methods.

The prospect of an early return of the Whigs to power, on the split in the Tory Party over the repeal of the Corn Laws, brought to a head the inherent opposition between the Romantic Nationalism of the Young Irelanders and O'Connell's more utilitarian brand. To the young men the direct pursuit of Repeal was a sacred duty. There must be no regressions and no trucking with any British governments, Tory or Whig, if opposed to Repeal. To renew the Whig Alliance would be a betrayal of the Repeal Association, a dereliction of the national ideal. To O'Connell the renewal was common sense. Each concession wrung from the British would be a weakening of the Union, a step on the road to Repeal, and he had always been ready to take half a loaf rather than knock his head against the bakery wall.

But the Young Irelanders were not motivated solely by an undue concern with ideology. They knew that O'Connell's alliance with the Whigs had lasted six years, from 1835 to 1841. Admittedly, he had founded the Repeal Association in 1840, but he had not begun to pursue Repeal energetically until 1842. How long might another Whig alliance last? Even middle-aged Repealers, not only ardent young men, might wonder in what direction O'Connell's political affections really lay. Today, we know from hundreds of his private letters that he was deeply committed to Repeal, but the Young Irelanders could only judge by what they saw him say and do.

There was another cause of irritation. Though the Young Irelanders' unofficial organ, *The Nation*, was widely read, its editorials and articles were published anonymously and thus brought no popular renown to their authors. Their only means of becoming widely known as individuals was through their speeches at the weekly meetings of the Repeal Association. Their direct political influence extended little beyond the middle classes of Dublin and the principal towns. There was only one nationally known figure among them — William Smith O'Brien — and he owed his celebrity more to his social position as a Protestant aristocrat and to his pleasant personality than to political ability. No matter how able or intelligent or eloquent the Young Irelanders, O'Connell could always appeal over their heads to the country at large. He was the national leader, the Man of the People, his influence permeating all sections of the nationalist population. Consequently the young men were frustrated, and they longed to assert themselves and their ideas in the face of the powerful old man.

An additional irritation to which, in my opinion, far too much importance has been attached, is the personality and activities of O'Connell's favourite son John. In this context historians have been influenced by Charles Gavan Duffy's self-serving *Four Years of Irish History, 1845-1849* which maintained that Young Irelanders might have put up with the old man's alleged prevarication and intolerance but were provoked beyond endurance by what was considered his son's arrogance and pretensions. John was provocative but his role in the controversy over the Whig Alliance and that leading up to the introduction of the Peace Resolutions was a minor one. During the first six months of 1846 he was most of the time in London attending Parliament, and was present at only five of the twenty- six weekly public meetings of the Repeal Association in Dublin. He spoke only twice at any length and only once on a controversial topic — on the Colleges bill on 19 January. He attended the meeting on 6 July, at which O'Connell introduced important measures, but did not speak. He did make some irritating comments during the debate on the Peace Resolutions on 13 July but was completely overshadowed by his father. The assertion that John was instrumental in provoking the Young Irelanders into engaging O'Connell in a confrontation that might otherwise have been avoided, cannot be sustained.

The Young Irelanders frequently asserted in the Repeal Association that they were being denied freedom to express their opinions. The frequency with which they made these assertions, however, weakens their case and suggests that, in fact, they were allowed considerable latitude. This was perceived by Frederick Lucas, the owner-editor of the English Catholic review, *The Tablet*, and the only Englishman to support Repeal. In an editorial on 18 July 1846, he charged the young men with behaviour over recent months which he considered disruptive and disloyal to the Repeal Association; and he warned them that conduct like theirs would not have been tolerated in the Anti-Corn Law League in England.

Though Lucas saw the outlines of the Irish political picture, he may have failed to discern the more vivid coloring. The Young Irelanders did have a case. It arose from the fact that O'Connell sometimes behaved as if he were independent of the Association and not bound by its resolutions. There was, admittedly, a certain realism in this. As the accepted national leader and as a politician of vast experience and proved ability, he could scarcely be expected to allow his judgment and conduct to be circumscribed by the decisions of an organization whose members were remote from London, the centre of political power.

The outstanding example of this independence was his handling of the Dungarvan by-election in June-July 1846. The Repeal Association had decided to put up Repeal candidates in every constituency in which there was a reasonable hope of having them elected. When the borough of Dungarvan, Co. Waterford, fell vacant it was expected that a Repealer would be nominated and probably returned. O'Connell deliberately delayed the nomination of a Repealer until it was too late. In consequence, his old friend and former political colleague, Richard Lalor Sheil, Ireland's leading Catholic Whig, was elected unopposed on 11 July, two days before the debate on the Peace Resolutions. Given the renewal of the Whig alliance, Sheil's election was a virtual necessity: he would be O'Connell's 'hot line' to the incoming Whig prime minister. To the Young Irelanders, however, the Dungarvan affair could only be seen as double-dealing on O'Connell's part.

The hostility to any new combination with the Whigs first appeared, and in no uncertain manner, when William Smith O'Brien wrote O'Connell a letter in December 1845. He called for a policy of neutrality in regard to the British Whigs and Tories: good measures should be supported and bad ones opposed no matter which party sponsored them; and the Irish nation should not be placed 'under the feet of the English Whigs.'[19] In his reply O'Connell somewhat deviously expressed his complete agreement with O'Brien's request, though he was careful to describe the policy of neutrality as pertaining to the coming session of Parliament — a hint that he considered this neutrality a matter of tactics rather than principle. His true attitude to party roles was indicated at the end of his reply:

> If we could have managed to play our cards well in Lord John's [proposed Whig] Government, we should have squeezed out a great deal of good for Ireland without for one moment merging or even postponing Repeal but on the contrary advancing that measure. Every popular concession, as I know, advances the cause of Repeal. I could satisfy you on this point and will when we meet.[20]

Smith O'Brien's anxiety was shared by many others. On 20 December, *The Nation* attacked the Whigs. A week later it renewed its attack and expressed scorn for any man who would accept an offer of food as a substitute for Repeal, a reference to the famine of 1845. At a banquet in February 1846 of the '82 Club' — an organization in which Young Irelanders rather than O'Connellites predominated— several of the young men condemned any suggestion of close cooperation with the Whigs.[21]

The hostility to the alliance was more vigorously expressed in the following month, March 1846, by Thomas Francis Meagher at the Repeal Association. He expressed disdain for the Whig Administration of 1835-41 which he alleged had a corrupting effect on Irishmen whom it bribed with government appointments:

> We have recovered and grown strong since their [the Whigs'] defeat in '41 and if at some future period they return to office, they shall find us a reformed people, too honest to be bribed, too powerful to be crushed (hear, hear, and cheers).[22]

The Young Irelanders did not dare attack O'Connell's leadership openly since he was still the popular idol, but they could pursue that objective by expressing scorn for the Whigs with whom O'Connell had been so closely and so publicly identified. Meagher returned to the assault a month later with a long speech at the Repeal Association in which he said,

> We asked for justice, withdrawing our demand for independence. What then? We submitted to the Union, we recognized the English Parliament as the trustee of Irish interests, and we must now submit to the consequences of that recognition — national discomfiture, national dishonour (hear, hear). . . . The true nationalist aspires to legislative independence, will not stop short at legislative ameliora- tion (cheers). . . . Our object is Irish independence, not Whig reform (enthusiastic cheering).[23]

The next number of *The Nation* expressed approval of Meagher's speech.[24]

A new factor now provoked unrest in the Repeal Association. It arose from Smith O'Brien's refusal to serve on a House of Commons railway committee on the ground that he was an Irish MP and would only serve on committees dealing with Irish affairs. His refusal was declared to be illegal, and he was confined to the prison of the House of Commons for a month, from late April to late May. His action made him the hero of many, inside and outside the Repeal Association, and of the Young Irelanders in particular. They saw in his independent conduct the correct antidote to O'Connell's affection for the Whigs.

Smith O'Brien's imprisonment became an issue in the Repeal Asso- ciation in late April when one of the members, William Gernon, asked the chairman at the weekly meeting, O'Connell's faithful Thomas Steele, to call for three cheers for O'Brien. Steele refused, on the ground that it would be dangerous to applaud a man for an illegal act, whereupon Gernon called for the applause himself, and the meeting responded with 'enthusiastic cheers.'[25]

At the Association's meeting on 4 May, Michael Doheny, one of the older Young Irelanders, proposed a motion in honour of O'Brien (Doheny had toned down the original draft of his motion at the request of the O'Connellites, who feared expressing approval of an illegality).[26] The meeting adopted the motion, but an altercation took place between two supporters of O'Connell, Edward Clements and Thomas Steele, and the four Young Irelanders, Doheny, Thomas MacNevin, Richard O'Gorman, Jr., and Michael J. Barry.[27]

The Nation took the Association to task for its timid motion in honour of Smith O'Brien and compared its weak action with the courageous address voted by the '82 Club'.[28] The club had gone even further, by sending a deputation to London which presented the address to O'Brien. The deputation consisted of John Mitchel, Terence Bellew McManus, O'Gorman, Doheny, and Meagher.[29]

In a letter to the Repeal Association, read at its weekly meeting on 4 May, O'Connell expressed his admiration for O'Brien but was careful not to commit himself to approval of O'Brien's conduct concerning the railway committee.[30] This refusal to give firm support exacerbated relations between O'Connell and the young men, who now became more belligerent. They showed their disapproval by praising O'Brien and the late Thomas Davis exuberantly while either ignoring O'Connell or praising only his past achievements and his ability as leader. They were careful to attribute no virtue whatever to O'Connell while seeing noble qualities in O'Brien and Davis. Editorials in *The Nation* used the same tactic.

The first striking example of this new development occurred in a speech by Doheny to the Repeal Club of Liverpool, to a group of Irish workers. His discourse included the passage:

> I have never flattered Mr. O'Connell but I feel I estimate as proudly as any his true greatness (cheers). And estimating him thus, feeling that his name is a part of his country's glory, could I take pride in any course that is not his course? It is, it will be my pride to follow him, and if need be to die for him (loud and long continued cheering).[31]

Having made this obeisance to his leader, Doheny proceeded to praise physical force and to make it clear that he had no intention of following O'Connell's course (this part of his speech will be dealt with later in this study). In the Repeal Association a week later Doheny was even more extravagant in his praise of O'Connell, but the praise was all for past achievements, no mention being made of leadership in the future and no virtues attributed. The eulogy ended with a definite hint of trouble ahead:

> But I trust our great leader shall not the less estimate, or the less truly appreciate, the feelings of gratitude and respect which I entertain for him, because in the same bosom I entertain a feeling of respect for myself, and I cherish the highest respect for the expression of truth everywhere.[32]

The third notable instance of this ambivalent praise of O'Connell occurred in Richard O'Gortnan Jr.'s speech at the Repeal Association on 25 May. Having denied that the Young Irelanders felt any hostility to O'Connell he continued:

We have read much of Old and Young Ireland.... With the gentlemen supposed to constitute the latter party I have many opinions in common. They were the opinions of one [Thomas Davis] who is now no more, of one whose purity of purpose and brilliancy of genius, whose gentleness of heart, have earned for him the only reward he ever sought — the love and consideration of all who knew him.

O'Gorman went on to praise O'Connell's incomparable achievements for which he had won the gratitude of all, but then came the crunch:

But we owe a debt also to ourselves, that shall as truly and as surely be paid — to protect our own right of opinion — our independence of thought (cries of hear, hear, hear).[33]

At this meeting of the Association a third Young Irelander, Michael Joseph Barry, took the same line. Having, like O'Gorman, insisted that there was no dissension between Young Ireland and O'Connell he declared that 'we are enrolled under Mr O'Connell's leadership, and in every matter of detail — in everything which compromises no conscientious opinion of ours, we cheerfully follow his guidance.'[34] Barry then referred to Davis's quarrel with O'Connell (over the Colleges Bill in 1845) which was mended when Davis 'showed how noble and truly generous a heart was his.'[35] There was no suggestion that O'Connell's heart was either noble or generous, and the omission was obvious.

This tactic of ambivalent praise of O'Connell combined with whole-hearted praise of others drew the fire of *The Tablet*, the organ of that English Catholic supporter of Repeal, Frederick Lucas. On 16 May, *The Nation* had complimented Smith O'Brien on the fact that he did not 'lug' religious topics into the Repeal Association's discussions. The reference was clearly meant as a censure of O'Connell who frequently introduced such topics. *The Tablet* of the following week — 23 May — expressed its concern:

It is impossible to see without regret the attempts that are being made to exalt Mr O'Brien's character and achievements above those of Mr O'Connell. And not merely so but to place his general character, his trustworthiness, and, above all, his position with regard to religious questions, on a higher eminence than those of the Liberator.... Mr O'Connell is dispraised by the negatives used to eulogise Mr O'Brien.[36]

In response to a disclaimer from *The Nation* on 30 May, *The Tablet* repeated its censure on 6 June, and added the comment: 'A more bitter and unhandsome attack upon O'Connell . . . it has rarely fallen to our lot to peruse.'[37]

The Nation renewed its attack on O'Connell, on 30 May, with an editorial entitled, 'Smith O'Brien.' The final paragraph was so important that it must be quoted in full:

> As to deposing O'Connell from the Leadership of the Irish People we have met with no man insane enough to propose or contemplate that. The thing is not possible. O'Connell wields the Irish millions, and he alone — he has wielded them for forty years; and we know of no man, or set of men, able to wrest the leading-staff out of his hand. Whithersoever, how far soever the Irish Nation goes, he will be at their head to his dying day. All we mean to insist upon is this — that we will be led to the goal whither we are bound; we will not go back, or stand still: we will be led, but it must be *forward*. O'Connell is our leader, and must remain our leader; he has mighty power, mighty responsibility: let him lead us, in God's name — and full sure we are he will not lead a trusting people astray, to his own eternal peril and our ignominious defeat and destruction.[38]

The praise rings false. *The Nation* is testifying to O'Connell's power but to nothing else. The message comes through that he is not to be trusted. The final sentence is a threat in the form of a compliment.

On 6 June *The Nation* all but came out openly against O'Connell, with an editorial comment in the form of a rhetorical question: 'As they advance to Repeal, will any coward or slave amongst us sneak back to Whiggism, or precursorism, or some other wretched form of *halfness* accursed of gods and men.' 'Precursorism' was a reference to the Precursor Society which O'Connell founded in 1838 as a forerunner to the inauguration of the Repeal movement.

On the same day, 6 June, a number of Whig MPs met at Lord John Russell's London house and discussed how best to oppose Peel's Irish coercion bill, now in its later stages through the House of Commons.[39] O'Connell, his son John, and some other Repeal MPs were present — a strong hint that the Whig Alliance was being renewed. The Unionist *Dublin Evening Mail* put a cat among the pigeons by reporting that O'Connell had said at this meeting that 'all he ever wished, with respect to the Legislative Union, was that it should be a real union — real in the equality of laws, franchises, privileges, in both countries.'[40] There was nothing surprising in this statement, if he made it, and he probably did. Throughout his public life he had constantly declared that he would

abandon Repeal if the British government were to make the Union a
reality, by giving Ireland good government. This declaration made useful
propaganda in Britain, appealing to Whigs and Radicals prepared to
cooperate with him on Irish reforms. But he was convinced that no British
government ever would or could give Ireland that kind of rule. He was
writing a check which he was certain would never be presented for
payment. The Young Irelanders must have known that the statement now
attributed to him by the *Dublin Evening Mail* was merely a repetition of
what he had always said, but they affected to believe otherwise.[41]

A few days later *The Nation* had two editorials attacking the renewal of
the Whig alliance. In the second it denied that O'Connell had said at the
Whig meeting in Russell's house that 'all he wanted ever was a real Union
— the same laws, the same franchises', and so forth. It considered that he
would have been incapable of saying such a thing.[42]

In the Repeal Association on 15 June Meagher delivered a stinging
attack on O'Connell, not directly but by the familiar method of attacking
the Whigs:

> The suspicion is abroad that the national cause will be sacrificed to
> Whig supremacy, and that the people who are now striding on to
> freedom will be purchased back into factious vassalage (hear, hear).
> . . . But on their return to power the Whigs shall find that in their
> absence you have become a reformed people. They shall find that
> you have abjured the errors of faction and have been instructed in the
> truths of patriotism [that] you have vowed never more to act the
> Sepoy for English faction (loud cheers). To their reproach, Sir, it must
> be said that the people of this country have been too long the
> credulous menials of English liberalism.[43]

There followed a witty and sarcastic denunciation of the Whig administration of 1835-41 that was as insulting (by implication) to O'Connell as
it was grossly unfair to Mulgrave, Morpeth and Drummond. Each barb
was greeted by such reactions as 'laughter', 'renewed laughter', and 'roars
of laughter'. O'Connell had always encouraged Catholics to take office in
order to shake the Protestant monopoly of power, and Meagher now
attacked this policy with the statement: 'You have learned to regard a Whig
Government in Ireland as little else than a state relief committee for Irish
political mendicants.'

O'Gorman and Mitchel spoke in support of Meagher at this meeting.
Both denied that the Repeal Association could ever desert Repeal for a
Whig alliance, Mitchel insisting that O'Connell had not said that he would
accept a real union.

At the next meeting of the Association — on 22 June — a letter was read from O'Connell which took the Young Irelanders to task:

> It is with bitterest regret and deepest sorrow that I witness the efforts which are made by some of our juvenile members to create dissensions, and circulate distractions among the Repealers. It is manifest that a majority of the Repeal Association must exert themselves strenuously to support the Association, or the persons to whom I allude will divide its ranks, and finally destroy the Association itself.[44]

Barry was the first of the young men to defend himself against these charges, and he went on to say,

> I do not forget that Mr O'Connell is the ablest of living Irishmen and that he has fought for half a century in Ireland's cause (cheers). . . . Sir, if this alleged announcement by Mr O'Connell, that he sought only a real union, were true — then Mr O'Connell, who has so long advocated the Repeal of the Union, so often declared that nothing but a Repeal of the Union can benefit and free Ireland — would be a cheat and a liar (cheers). The allegation as to Mr O'Connell is false.

Gorman likewise denied that he had been causing dissension, and he took the same line as Barry by asserting that O'Connell could not possibly have said that he was prepared to accept a real Union in place of Repeal. Had he said that, O'Connell would be no fit leader for the Repeal Association, no fit leader for the Irish people. Mitchel expressed his belief that 'Mr. O'Connell has not said or hinted in that letter that Repeal was to be sacrificed, or for one minute postponed, to facilitate Whig government.' Doheny, too, said that O'Connell would not renew the Whig alliance.[45]

In speeches and editorials the Young Irelanders had identified the renewal of that alliance with betrayal of Repeal, and had stated it as their conviction that O'Connell would not perpetrate such a deed. They had set a trap for him: it remained to see whether he would fall into it.

On 23 June Peel's Government was defeated on the second reading of the Irish Coercion Bill by a combination of Whigs, Protectionist Tories, and Repealers. Its resignation followed, and on 1 July Lord John Russell took office at the head of a Whig administration. The crisis had come: but the Young Irelanders were now to learn that O'Connell was a master of the political game. He crossed to Dublin and attended the weekly meeting of the Repeal Association on 6 July. There he outlined his intention of having the new Whig government enact eleven bills.

The bills provided for an extension of the parliamentary suffrage, a more thorough municipal reform, 'an act to give perfect freedom of education to every class and persuasion' (along religious denominational lines), the substitution in fiscal matters of elected county boards for the landlord-dominated grand juries, a radical reform of landlord-tenant relations (a subject O'Connell had been stressing for the previous eight months), and an absentee tax of 20% on rents. He asked the Association to adopt these measures so that he could return to London to try to have the Whig Government enact them. The Association did so, without a dissenting voice. The Young Irelanders present — Barry, Meagher, Mitchel, and O'Gorman — acquiesced in silence.[46]

It would be idle for the Repealers to expect the new government to undertake even part of this legislative programme unless they were ready to make a serious commitment to that government, that is, to renew the Whig alliance. That renewal was implicit in the Association's adoption of the eleven bills.

The tables had been turned. The attack on the Whig alliance had not only been repulsed but to keep up that attack any longer would leave the Young Irelanders open to the charge that they were refusing to join O'Connell in his campaign for agrarian and political reform, that they were indifferent to the welfare of the people.[47] In the hands of an astute politician that charge could be used with devastating effect. O'Connell had only to exploit it if his primary purpose was the rout of the Young Irelanders. Not only did he neglect to exploit it but, instead, he switched the debate in the following week to the Peace Resolutions. He would now have to fight the young men all over again, but this time on difficult terrain. They would be able to appeal to the martial ardour of a people known for their physical courage, to a folk-memory inured to violence.

In the first week of July O'Connell had demonstrated his mastery of the political art: in the second week — if his essential aim was the defeat of the young men — he exhibited the quality of an incompetent amateur. Can these two apparently contradictory roles be reconciled? They can: but only by accepting the explanation that O'Connell's primary object was not the defeat of the Young Irelanders but the preservation of the moral force principle.

The decks had now been cleared for action. At the next meeting of the Repeal Association, on 13 July, O'Connell would introduce the Peace Resolutions and commence the debate which would rage for the rest of 1846. Before considering these resolutions, however, it is necessary to go back over the previous nine months to trace the attitude of the Young Irelanders to violence.

In an editorial in October 1845 *The Nation* demonstrated an ability to say contrary things at the same time. It lauded Ireland 'for which the great Chiefs fought and died. Ireland whose name rung above the roar of battle in all the stormy fields which shine in the history of southern Europe.' Then mindful of its allegiance to O'Connell it added:

> Remember *opinion* is your sole weapon. Force you must put out of the question. Mr O'Connell has declared that nothing will induce him to use it. If others propose it to you, you would promptly and wisely put them aside. It is by opinion alone you must conquer.

The editorial then returned to its first love by praising the Volunteers of 1782 for, 'when the earliest link of the Catholic chains were broken, the concession was granted under the guns of the Northern Volunteers' (a piece of historical nonsense).[48] Its fervour increased with a reference to the Rebellion of 1798:

> The spirit that struck for Ireland was begotten in Belfast, nurtured on the plains of Down and in the glens of Antrim, and baptised in blood in the streets of Ballynahinch. . . . A generous conciliation . . . [will] kindle anew the flame that burned in Ulster when Russell planned, and Porter preached, and Drennan sang, and Munroe fought, and McCracken died, for Ireland.[49]

The first of the Young Irelanders to express approval of physical force in the Repeal Association in 1846 was Richard O'Gorman, Jr. In his speech on 23 February, he managed to combine praise of both moral and physical force at the same time:

> You strive to win your freedom by the might of mind — by power of the intellect — by the energy of strong will (hear, hear, and cheers). Well and wisely have you chosen. . . . But, Sir, let none mistake me. God forbid that in this assembly of honest men I should dare to breathe one breath of censure against the memory of the men who fought in the ranks of freedom, and died to secure the liberties of man. Thank God, this attempt would be in vain, for their names are long since engraven deep on the true heart of man, and from around their tombs, as from holy altars, ever arise to heaven the orisons of grateful nations (hear and cheers). For the true benefactors of man are never by mankind forgotten.[50]

At the same meeting Barry made a long speech in which he lauded the Volunteers of 1782 and described the great blessings which a man's life can confer if that life is properly used; 'But when men tell us that life is not to be the means of securing for man these blessings, but that these are to be sacrificed to its preservation, then I for one arraign the doctrine as false and wicked (cheers).'[51]

In an editorial in April, entitled 'Poland and Ireland,' *The Nation* took the (English though pro-Repeal) *Tablet* to task for condemning the recent Polish revolution as rash and unjustified. *The Nation* thought otherwise:

> If the late insurrection did no more than show that Poland still holds a living heart, . . . to do this was worth some blood. . . . We *believe* in the sentiment
>
>> That Freedom's battle, once begun,
>> bequeathed from bleeding sire to son
>> though baffled oft, is *ever won.*
>
> Better a little blood-letting — to show that there is blood — than a patient dragging of chains.[52]

The praise of physical force became a more serious matter on 16 May when Doheny made his speech to the Repealers in Liverpool, to which reference has already been made. After pledging his loyalty to O'Connell's leadership Doheny went on to say:

> There is a fearful moral obligation on man not to go to war unless war is necessary. There is no greater evil than unnecessary war. But I hold as doctrine that there are times when both obligations are to be set at nought, and when the strength of man, contending for principle, must be decided by the issue of his own blood (cheers). . . . Understand me as uttering not the thoughts that come now, but the feelings which I have shared with the men [the Young Irelanders] in whose faith and courage I have intimate trust (loud cheers).[53]

George Archdeacon, the sub-secretary of the Liverpool Repeal Club,[54] responded to Doheny's address with a statement which included the passage:

> They felt their position there, and they were prepared, even with their physical strength, if necessary, to defend their principles (cheers). They were a powerful body in Liverpool, and formed into solid squares, they would beat two millions of Saxons (hear, hear).

At the weekly meeting of the Repeal Association on 1 June O'Connell brought up the matter of Archdeacon's speech at the Liverpool meeting.

He considered the speech left the Association open to a charge of sedition and called for his expulsion from the organization. He put two Resolutions to the meeting — they were both passed — one for the expulsion of Archdeacon, the other a renewal of the Association's pledge to use only moral force:

> That the principle upon which this Association always sought, and seeks, the restoration of the Irish Parliament, is the principle of perfectly peaceful, legal and constitutional exertion, and none other.[55]

George Archdeacon was nobody of importance, and the British Government was unlikely to bother about a Repeal speech, however seditious, made in England. O'Connell obviously picked on the event to have the moral force principle reaffirmed. By concentrating on Archdeacon and ignoring Doheny, whose speech was much more likely to make converts to violence, O'Connell must have been trying to avoid a confrontation with the Young Irelanders, at least for the present.

He had now induced the Repeal Association to pledge its allegiance once again to moral force, just six months since it had last done so — in January 1846. But the reaffirmation was soon undone by an editorial in *The Nation* and by two speeches in the Association.

The Nation published its editorial on 27 June. It was an open challenge to the principle of moral force:

> True it is, that we and others do differ in theory from Mr O'Connell as to the relative values of national liberty and individual life. We think scarcely any amount of the latter equivalent to the former. Mr. O'Connell thinks each priceless. We think the means used by Hofer, by Washington, by Tell, by Kosciusko, are not means unfit for Christian men, or brave men, or honest men to use. We think the object affects the means — that to war for national existence is not infamous. . . . And while we respect Mr O'Connell's opinion, we maintain our own. . . . [In 1782 Grattan] thundered . . . to thousands of armed Volunteers, and Ireland was free.

On 29 June Smith O'Brien attended the weekly meeting of the Repeal Association for the first time since his imprisonment. He delivered a good-humored rebuke to the organization for its neglect to give him adequate support on the railway committee issue, and devoted the bulk of his speech to a denunciation of the renewal of the Whig Alliance. He demanded that members be allowed to express their opinions freely:

> No man who joins this Association is committed to any opinion

which may be pronounced by any other individual, or by even the committee of the Association, or by the Association itself (hear). I believe I speak not only in accordance with the rules of the Association, but in accordance with that which is interpreted as its doctrine, that no man who joins the Association is thereby pledged to any opinion except a determination to obtain domestic legislation for Ireland (cheers).[56]

In view of the reaffirmation of moral force as a fundamental principle of the Association on June 1 and the very pointed editorial in *The Nation* on men's rights to differ from O'Connell on moral force on 27 June, O'Brien's speech could only be interpreted by the reading public[57] as a polite but firm denial that that principle was part of the constitution of the Association. At the Association the previous week, O'Gorman had made short work of the contention that moral force was anything more than a policy of the organization:

I know this Association has laws — laws to which, as a member, I am bound to conform. I know one of these laws is that we are to seek the attainment of our object by strictly peaceable means — by moral force (hear, hear) — and I, for one, am here to strive that it be fully and fairly tried (cheers). My own opinions regarding physical force and its merits I have therefore, of course, no need to set before you here; but if another man chooses to put forward his opinions on the subject — if he casts what I believe an undeserved aspersion on the memory of great and good men, who have battled of old for freedom and died fighting for the cause of man, then, Sir, I respectfully say I do not agree with him, and that I, for one, respect their memory as sacred and I think they acted nobly and well (enthusiastic cheers).[58]

If O'Connell were to take no action in light of these declarations, he must accept the contention that moral force was no longer a fundamental principle of the Repeal Association. So he decided on action. He crossed to Ireland and removed the matter of the Whig Alliance as a threat to his leadership with the adoption by the Association of the eleven bills. He was then free to face the Young Irelanders on the issue of violence.

On 11 July he placed a document — soon to be known as the Peace Resolutions — before the General Committee of the Repeal Association. This document recited various declarations on moral force adopted by the Association at different times in the past — at its foundation in April 1840; in November 1840; September 1841; November 1843; September 1844; and January 1846. All these declarations insisted that moral force, constitutional methods, and non-violence were fundamental to the Association. Having made this recital the document added these four paragraphs:

> Having thus detailed the reiteration of the principles of action adopted by the Association, being in itself the very basis of the Association — namely, the principle that the amelioration of political institutions ought not be sought for by any other means than those which are perfectly peaceable, legal, and constitutional.
>
> That to promote political amelioration, peaceable means alone should be used, to the exclusion of all others save those that are peaceable, legal, and constitutional.
>
> It has been said very unwisely that this principle prohibits the necessary defence against unjust aggression on the part of a domestic government, or a foreign enemy. It does no such thing. It leaves the right of self-defence perfectly free to the use of any force sufficient to resist and defeat unjust aggression.
>
> We emphatically announce our conviction that all political amelioration — and the first, and highest of all, the Repeal of the Union — ought to be sought for, and can be sought for successfully only by peaceable, legal, and constitutional means, to the utter exclusion of any other. In short, that the Repeal of the Union can, and ought, to be obtained by the same peaceable means by which Catholic Emancipation was achieved, and by the same exclusively peaceable system of action by which the Anti-Corn Law League so gloriously triumphed over every resistance, and obtained the repeal of the corn laws. By such means alone we can — we ought — and, with the blessing of Almighty Providence, we will obtain the Repeal of the Union.[59]

The third paragraph proves that O'Connell was not asking his followers to pledge themselves to pacificism.

In a discussion of the Resolutions in the General Committee O'Connell 'distinctly stated' their intention to be 'that the abstract principle of disclaiming physical force in any event must be held by all members of the Association.' The Committee adopted the Resolutions, Mitchel and Meagher alone dissenting.[60]

At the weekly meeting of the Association two days later, 13 July, O'Connell introduced the Resolutions by declaring:

> I tell you that I want you to declare fairly either for my principles or against them. I want you to declare for the principle of peaceful, but

continuous agitation — of that agitation which alone deserves success, and which, in my conscience, I am convinced can alone obtain it — I want you to declare for me in that or for the admission of the fiendish nonsense which suggests physical force and violent achievement (cheers). . . . The achievement of our liberties, and the amelioration of our condition, by peaceable and legal means, is the first principle of my political life. I am going to test that principle today.[61]

The Young Irelanders who took part in the debate were Meagher, Mitchel, and O'Gorman. The important and relevant parts of the debate can be reduced to quotable excerpts.

Meagher described his position:

I agree that no other means should be adopted in the Association but moral means, and peaceful means; but if you determine that it is futile and that Repeal cannot be carried by such means, then I am prepared to adopt another policy — a policy no less honourable though it may be more perilous — a policy which I cannot disclaim as inefficient or immoral, for greater names have sanctioned its adoption, and noble events have attested its efficiency.

Mitchel said:

Before you put the question I desire to say a few words — not that I mean to oppose the resolutions. In so far as they disclaim on the part of the society all intention of resorting to arms, I cordially concur in them. And as for the abstract and universal principle which seems to be contained in them, the principle that no national or political rights ought at any time, or under any circumstances, or by any people, to be sought for with an armed hand, I content myself with saying that I do not approve of that principle. I do not abhor, for instance, the Volunteers of 1782 (hear) who took up arms to procure a political amelioration, and would have deemed it cheaply purchased by a river of blood.

He went on to cite the American Revolution and the Irish Rebellion of 1798 in support of his refusal to accept moral force as an abstract and universal principle.

Meagher and Mitchel had now made it clear that they had no objection in principle to the use of physical force to attain great and desirable political ends. Mitchel was trying to alter the meaning of the Peace

Resolutions when he said that they seemed to comprise the 'abstract and universal principle' that 'no national or political rights ought at any time, or under any circumstances, or by any people, to be sought for with an armed hand.' The Resolutions contained no such assertion. In seeing them as having a universal application Mitchel may well have been influenced by O'Connell's words spoken to the General Committee that 'the abstract principle of disclaiming physical force in any event must be held by all members of the Association.' But even these words did not have the universal meaning that Mitchel was attributing to the Peace Resolutions. If spoken to an academic audience the words might be held to refer to nations and states in general — applied to an oriental despotism they might be ridiculous — but instead, they were spoken by an Irish politician to an Irish political committee concerned with Irish politics. To see them as having a universal application was to go beyond the limits of common sense.

In response to Mitchel's argument that he could not agree to any condemnation of George Washington, O'Connell (taking some liberties with American history) said that 'Washington bravely defended his country from aggression and won its independence, and that principle we not only recognise but are prepared to act upon.' Mitchel's remarks about the Volunteers of 1798 provoked O'Connell into expostulating:

> Now, am I not called upon to interfere? (hear, hear). What can this man's object be? He purports to be a man of peace, and yet he preaches of war; he affects to advocate moral and tranquil courses, and yet his speech has the direct tendency to instigating the country to anarchy and violence (hear, hear).... Are we then to be humbugged by this species of pretended acquiescence and real difference?

In reply to a repetition by Mitchel of his statement that he dissented from the Resolutions in so far as they 'convey, or seem to convey' a general condemnation of 'other societies and other people', O'Connell said: 'I drew up this resolution to draw a marked line between Young Ireland and Old Ireland (cheers). I do not accept the services of any man who does not agree with me both in theory and in practice.'

The third Young Irelander, O'Gorman, stated his views towards the end of the debate:

> Mr. O'Gorman could not say that he abhorred physical force or thought an appeal to arms at all times, and under all circumstances, unworthy and criminal. It was obvious to every one that the use of physical force was in this land, and under existing circumstances,

impracticable and absurd (hear, hear). He was the last man to in-
culcate anything of the kind. However, he could not go to the full
length of admitting 'abhorrence' of that power which other times and
other circumstances had often before now rendered feasible and
successful (hear).

O'Connell replied: 'He will not be bound by the resolutions. If he is not,
he cannot be a member of the Association.' O'Gorman came back with,
'I say, I am bound by them.'

When the chairman put the adoption of the Peace Resolutions to the
meeting they were carried 'amidst deafening acclamations'. Meagher was
reported as the only man to say 'No', and O'Connell cried out, 'There is
one solitary "No".'

In the debate O'Connell was obliged to define the moral force principle
verbally in as uncompromising a form as possible. Only by doing so could
he force the Young Irelanders to declare themselves openly and without
further equivocation. Once the moral force principle had been accepted in
this very special and unambiguous way, and after such an important
debate, it could be used to expel any members who continued to question
it as fundamental to the Repeal Association. This was made clear when he
said;

> I will not allow any person to take advantage of these resolutions.
> They must agree to them fully and unconditionally; and if I find any
> man violating those rules, I will appeal at once to the Association,
> and call for his ignominious expulsion (cheers).

That one of his aims (but not his primary aim) in proposing the Peace
Resolutions was to defeat or expel the Young Irelanders is clear also from
his letters. In writing to a political colleague in Kilkenny he said, 'Young
Meagher is calculated to do extreme mischief to the Repeal cause. He will
break up the Repeal Association unless I am able to prevent him.'[62] To
Smith O'Brien (not present at the debate on the Peace Resolutions), he
wrote:

> It is impossible for me to act with any of the avowed Young Irelanders
> unless they retract their physical force opinions . . . altogether and
> submit to the resolutions of the Association. I for one do not think I
> go too far in requiring the Young Irelanders candidly to adopt them
> or to cease to cooperate with us.[63]

As stated in the early part of this study, virtually all modern historians
agree that O'Connell used the Peace Resolutions as an expedient in order

to expel the young men. This interpretation rests in the main on two premises. The first is that the attack on the Whig Alliance was in itself a serious danger to O'Connell's leadership; and the second, that the young men had no intention of taking to violence in the forseeable future. Consequently, there was no need to introduce the Resolutions. On these points comment must be made.

The attack on the Whig Alliance was never as dangerous to O'Connell as the Young Irelanders believed and as historians have thought. It was useful propaganda while the Tories were in power but, once the Whigs returned to office, the resourceful O'Connell knew how to rally support for the alliance, by introducing his programme of reform in the eleven bills.

While it is true that the young men had no intention of taking up arms in the forseeable future (O'Connell never accused them of having such an intention), it is also true that their praise of violence in the Repeal Association and the columns of *The Nation* could not fail to have practical consequences in a land where violence was endemic. The large circulation of *The Nation* and the cheers which greeted the praise of violence in the Association were ominous signs. If the Repeal movement were to remain constitutional there was a real necessity to see that moral force was reaffirmed once again as a fundamental principle, but this time with such clarity as to rule out all further controversy. The Young Irelanders must either accept that principle unequivocally or get out.

In his *Four Years of Irish History*, Charles Gavan Duffy makes the charge that in proclaiming the Peace Resolutions O'Connell was throwing away a strategic advantage: British governments could discount the Repeal movement in the future since it would no longer carry the threat of revolutionary violence. The charge lacks weight because it overlooks both O'Connell's reputation in Britain and his years. Most British politicians distrusted him and were slow to believe anything he said. To Peel he was a scoundrel and to most Whig cabinet ministers, despite the Whig Alliance, a person with whom they would rather not have to deal. And what of those Whigs and Radicals who thought him sincere? Could they be sure that this aging Irishman would be able to control the passions of his countrymen in the future as in the past? The London *Times* saw the Resolutions as the attempt of an old man to stem the tide of violence which he himself had created, and it believed he would fail.[64] The strategic advantage O'Connell threw away did not amount to much.

Historians have not given due importance to O'Connell's knowledge of violence; perhaps because they have not stopped to consider the man he really was. He knew his people. Fostered out to a small farmer in accordance with Gaelic custom, he grew up with a close understanding of all classes of the Catholic population. Through the years and even as an old man he maintained intimate contact with ordinary people and in Kerry every autumn delighted in their company. In whatever part of the country he found himself and in Dublin, he never lost the common touch. As a brilliantly successful advocate he was defence counsel in a thousand cases involving charges of violence and membership of secret societies. He must have known more of these subjects than any other public man of his time. His views on Irish violence deserve greater respect than they have received.

6

O'Connell and his family

The Barony of Iveragh forms the western end of the peninsula that runs out from Killarney into the Atlantic. It is mountainous and weather-beaten tourist country, of bays and coves and beautiful views, separated from the rest of Kerry by a solid range of mountains. In O'Connell's day it was a thickly populated area of small holdings where farmers cut their turf and supplemented their incomes by sea fishing and by grazing cattle and sheep on the mountains. It was also a region in which the Gaelic language survived among all classes into the nineteenth century. Surviving also were a number of Gaelic and Catholic landowning families — McCarthys, O'Connells, O'Mahonys and Sugrues — though their significance owed more to lineage and 'following' than to material wealth.

The O'Connells were the principal family in the barony for some centuries before Daniel O'Connell was born in 1775. The head of the family was his uncle, Muiris a' Chaipín, known to posterity as Hunting-Cap. This uncle enormously expanded his inherited land by farming, smuggling, lending money, hard bargaining and, above all, by thrift. By 1800 he was rich in both land and securities. Hunting-Cap's brother Morgan did likewise, though on a more modest scale and more humanely. In addition, he ran a general store, reared ten children, of whom Daniel was the eldest son, and died prosperous.

Being born into a family that had both lineage and financial success was important to the development of O'Connell's personality. Impoverished lineage can be a millstone, encouraging a man to substitute fancies of ancient grandeur for hard work and honest ambition. He feels deprived, and consequently comes easily to hate and envy success. O'Connell's family background, combining lineage with economic expansion, placed him above the reach of these temptations: he could look the British Government and the Irish Protestant Ascendancy straight in the face without feeling impelled to hate the former and to envy and feel inferior to the latter.

His mother was a daughter of John O'Mullane, a small Catholic landlord near Mallow, Co. Cork, described as 'Chief of his Name'.[1] His mother's sister had married Nicholas Nagle of Castletherry, Mitchelstown, Co. Cork, a first cousin of Edmund Burke. The connection is interesting in that O'Connell seems to have had no regard whatever for that great statesman. He probably could not forgive Burke for his absolute condemnation of the French Revolution and his defence of the English landed aristocracy.

In 1802 O'Connell risked his prospects as the adopted son and heir of his rich but childless uncle, Hunting-Cap, by making an impecunious marriage. His bride was his distant cousin, Mary O'Connell, one of the eleven children of a Tralee physician who had died comparatively young. Mary was the daughter of a 'mixed' marriage, her mother a Catholic, her father a member of the Church of Ireland. In accordance with the custom of the time she and her sisters were reared as Catholics, her brothers as Protestants. When the ambitious Hunting-Cap learned that his promising young barrister nephew had married a girl without a dowry he 'wept with rage' and disinherited him. Some years later, however, he became reconciled to the erring young man and eventually bequeathed him a third of his wealth including Derrynane, the ancestral family home.

In those days the possession of a dowry, even though she had to hand it over to her husband, gave a woman self-respect. Mary was deeply sensitive on the point because, as late as 1825, after twenty-three years of marriage and the birth of eleven children, she could still say to her husband, when recommending that her brother Maurice's widow be employed as housekeeper at Derrynane: 'I feel now delicate in mentioning her to you as I have that feeling about me (it is pride I believe) not to have any of my family living at your expense when I brought you no *fortune*'.[2] Owing to the poverty of her widowed mother Mary's education was defective. She did not know French, and resented the superior airs of the family governess who had a very good knowledge of that language which was considered essential to a lady's education. Mary's brother Rickard shared this feeling of inferiority which he expressed in writing to congratulate O'Connell in 1815 on his escape from death in the duel with D'Esterre. Despite the fact that he had held a commission in the British Army and was currently an officer in the Kerry Militia, Rickard ended his letter with the apology: 'Make allowances for my manner of writing. You know my education was rather limited'.[3] There was no need for this self-deprecation since the letter was well written. Likewise, Mary wrote intelligent letters which, politics apart, are more interesting than her husband's.

Despite Hunting-Cap's wealth and Morgan O'Connell's success in business, life in Iveragh was modest. The Big Houses of the barony were physically small, Derrynane being a very large rambling farmhouse, the original part dating from shortly after 1700. The only house which the more fertile parts of Ireland would have described as a 'gentleman's residence' was the handsome late Georgian Castlequin (now a ruin), overlooking Cahirciveen and built by the Mahony family, probably in the early nineteenth century. An insight into the ruggedness in living standards of even so long-established and so prosperous a family as the O'Connells is gained from a letter in which O'Connell tells his future wife that, on hearing of their match, his sister Ellen expressed delight: 'She was always afraid', she said, 'that I would marry a proud woman of fashion who would look down on my family and despise this wild country'.[4]

O'Connell's six sisters married, all but Ellen by family arrangement, at least one having to marry a man she disliked.[5] The five parentally approved husbands were Catholics of modest landed property, one (William Finn) a son of a wealthy Carlow merchant who was sometime owner of Finn's *Leinster Journal* in Kilkenny. At least two of these husbands were of ancient family — Jeremiah McCartie of Woodview, Newmarket, Co. Cork and Daniel O'Sullivan of Reendonegan (the house is today just barely standing), Bantry, Co. Cork. Ellen kicked over the traces and married her kinsman, a Daniel O'Connell who was a Protestant attorney in Tralee of unsavoury reputatton. Her parents were all the more chagrined at her rebellion because another kinsman, also named Daniel O'Connell — he owned both the Great and Small Skelligs — was interested in her but she gave her heart to the attorney. Her marriage was the only one of the six that is known to have come unstuck. As a grass widow she kept house for Hunting-Cap at Derrynane, and ended her days nursing the sick poor with the Presentation Sisters in Cork city.

O'Connell's brother Maurice, his companion at school in St Omer and Douai, became lieutenant in Count Walsh de Serrant's regiment in the British Army, in what was known as 'Pitt's Irish Brigade'. This brigade was organised by the boys' uncle, General Count Daniel O'Connell, a royalist refugee from the French Revolution, and included many Irishmen who had been army officers under Louis XVI. Maurice died of fever on active service in San Domingo in 1797.

The next brother, John, acceded to Hunting-Cap's wishes by marrying a Co. Cork heiress, Elizabeth Coppinger. John lived as a 'country gentleman' at Grenagh (it still stands) near Killarney. His pack of staghounds was famous, and he amused himself even more destructively by fighting eighteen duels. However, he faced up to his responsibilities as a landlord during the Famine. He died bankrupt in 1853, but fortunately for his family his wife's property was tied up so that he could not squander it.

O'Connell's third and youngest brother, James, was a disciple of Hunting-Cap, more humane than his uncle though probably less cultured (Hunting-Cap's letters were Augustan prose spiced with apt quotations from the Latin classics). James pleased his uncle by marrying a girl with a dowry of £2,000, a daughter of O'Donoghue of the Glen, scion of perhaps Kerry's oldest family. The marriage took place no doubt in Killarney but it was honoured by an *aeríocht* (a community festival) at Derrynane, and by a song composed by the Iveragh poet, Tomás Ruadh Ó Súilleabháin, *Fáilte Shéamais' ac Mhurchada* (Welcome to Morgan's son James).

James looked after the pennies and nursed the lands he inherited from Hunting-Cap into a large estate. Though close-fisted he was good-natured and reluctantly lent money to his recklessly extravagant politician brother, accompanying each loan with warnings of doom which were invariably ignored. From about 1824 he lived at Lakeview near Killarney, replacing the modest old house there in 1870 with a much more ambitious one. Its special feature is the view from the reception rooms looking south over the magic of the Lower Lake. This uncharacteristic expenditure justified itself sixty years later when the money had run out and James's decendants turned the house into a successful hotel.

James was a Tory in politics but he switched allegiance in 1868 on learning that he would receive a baronetcy if Kerry returned two Liberal MPs in the general election of that year, Gladstone's decision to disestablish the Church of Ireland being the big issue. James worked hard in the Liberal interest and collected his prize in the following year.

Both the brothers John and James and their uncle, Count O'Connell, disapproved of the attempt to repeal the Act of Union. However, John compromised somewhat by subsidizing the successful election of his son Morgan John for Kerry in 1835. This son continued to represent Kerry until 1852. In 1865 he married Mary Anne Bianconi, daughter of the coaching magnate. As Mrs Morgan John O'Connell she wrote that historically valuable hotchpotch, *The Last Colonel of the Irish Brigade*.

O'Connell's relations with his wife and children have been ably described by Professor Helen Mulvey in an essay in the first volume of his correspondence. Consequently, I need only deal with those children when they grew up. There is, however, one aspect of O'Connell's life which needs further treatment since new knowledge has become available — his widespread reputation for sexual immorality. In her essay Professor Mulvey writes:

> On the subject of O'Connell's marital fidelity, on the accusations of Ellen Courtney and the later statements of Sir James O'Connor and W. B. Yeats, the letters [between O'Connell and his wife] have nothing explicit to say. But the substance and tone of the correspondence as a whole are powerful evidence of O'Connell's fidelity

and devotion to his wife and of his deep happiness in every aspect of his relationship with her.[6]

The letters do indicate that he sowed wild oats as a young man before his marriage but the charge is, rather, one of sustained adultery. No historian has found reliable evidence of infidelity but any statement to that effect is met by the popular rejoinder that everybody knows he was unfaithful. A solution to the mystery has now been suggested by the scholars of folklore. They depict O'Connell as the principal folk-hero of modern Irish history, and therein lies the root of this widespread belief. Diarmuid O Muirithe, who has studied the folklore on O'Connell, states:

> All over the country the people told stories of his fabulous virility. Rathkeale in Co. Limerick stands indicted as the only town that didn't provide a woman for his bed. His mistresses were legion and they included Queen Victoria. . . . These stories are products of the folk-mind. The heroes of old were ever famous for their sexual energy.[7]

This combination of history, correspondence and folklore points to the (disappointing?) conclusion that O'Connell was a faithful husband.

Of the eleven children born to O'Connell and Mary seven survived. They comprised four sons, Maurice, Morgan, John and Daniel, and three daughters, Ellen, Kate and Betsey. Considering the greatness of their father and the intelligence and resourcefulness of their mother the children were not very distinguished.

Maurice, the eldest son and the heir to the family property, was a brilliant student at Clongowes but he was lazy and failed to win a scholarship into Trinity College, Dublin. He studied at Trinity and in due time qualified as a barrister but did little professional practice. His father had him elected for Clare in 1831, and from 1832 until his death in 1853 he represented Tralee.

In 1832 Maurice made a romantic marriage, eloping in his yacht with Frances Scott from her home, Cahircon, on the Shannon estuary in West Clare. They were married in a Catholic ceremony in Tralee and a Protestant one in Kenmare. The Scotts were Cromwellian Protestant landlords of means but they sold out in the Encumbered Estates Court after the Famine. Cahircon is now a convent of the Salesian Sisters, and their other home, Knappogue in East Clare, a tourist banqueting castle.

Maurice and Frances had four children but then their marriage broke up. The O'Connell property was entailed so that the lazy and extravagant Maurice could not squander the capital. He spoke Irish[8] and was popular in Iveragh. He had illegitimate children, for at least one of whom his father was erroneously held responsible. In his *Four Years of Irish History 1845-1849* Charles Gavan Duffy maintains that Maurice sympathized with the Young Irelanders in their quarrel with O'Connell in 1846, but there is good reason to believe that Duffy is mistaken.[9]

O'Connell's second son, Morgan, was a lively and cheerful young man who went abroad to seek his fortune. When only fifteen-and-a-half years old he enlisted as an officer in the Irish Legion recruited to aid Bolivar in winning freedom for South America from Spanish rule. There is a portrait of him at Derrynane, probably painted by John Gubbins of Co Limerick. It depicts a comely, sensitive, earnest youth in the uniform of the Irish Legion. This force was organized by John Devereux of Co Wexford, an insurgent in 1798, who won O'Connell's enthusiastic backing for his expeditionary force for South America. Charges were made that Devereux was an adventurer who hoped to make a fortune — which he seems to have done — by organizing this force. Mr Eric T. D. Lambert, who is writing the history of the Irish Legion, considers that these charges contain a substantial amount of truth. O'Connell's correspondence shows that Devereux, however mistakenly, enjoyed his full trust.

O'Connell gave Morgan a letter for Bolivar which the young man delivered in person at Barranquilla, a Caribbean port in (modern) Colombia. O'Connell commenced his letter:

> Illustrious Sir,
> A stranger and unknown, I take the liberty of addressing you. I am encouraged to do so by my respect for your high character and by my attachment to that sacred cause which your talents, valour and virtue have gloriously sustained — I mean the cause of Liberty and national independence

The letter offered Morgan's 'humble but zealous exertions' and went on to compare Bolivar with Washington, 'your great prototype'.[10]

In his letter home reporting his presentation to Bolivar, Morgan wrote:

> He is a thin spare man about the height of my uncle Rick, very fine forehead, dark eyes and a very mild melancholy cast of countenance. He is a man of very reserved manners but, when he wishes, can be as merry as another.[11]

Morgan left South America for home in September 1821, fifteen months after his arrival there. In a letter to Hunting-Cap, O'Connell said of Morgan's departure:

The war is over in Colombia and, as he never intended to remain there unless with the chances which a continued warfare would give of exalted promotion, and especially as land, not money, is the mode of remunerating all services, he determined to come home.[12]

And what to do with Morgan now! O'Connell wished to make him an attorney but Mary would have none of it.

Now, love, to answer you on the subject of Morgan's becoming an attorney. I totally and entirely disapprove of it. It is a profession I never wished for any son of mine . . . [Morgan] is too fond of liberty ever to submit to the control of any person for a period of five years, much less consent to be bound to a *desk*. . . . It would be lost money to give him any other profession but the army.[13]

O'Connell could only reply that 'your advice with respect to Morgan is decisive'.[14] The young man wanted to enter the British service but O'Connell objected.[15] Count O'Connell recommended the Austrian Army as the most suitable,[16] and Morgan became a cadet in its 4th Regiment of Light Cavalry. Considering that he was a veteran of the French Army and had been promoted to the rank of a retired lieutenant-general after the Restoration, it is surprising that the Count did not suggest the French Army for Morgan. Unfortunately, in his letter on the subject he gives no reason for recommending the Austrian. Morgan was commissioned a lieutenant in the 6th Regiment of Light Cavalry while serving at Güns in Hungary in December 1826.[17] He does not seem to have made a success of his military career because he soon returned to Ireland where his father had him returned for Co. Meath in the general election of December 1832. He continued to sit for Meath until 1840 when he was appointed Assistant-Registrar of Deeds, and was Registrar from 1846 until his retirement in 1869. He had little interest in politics, and just did as his father directed. In 1840 he married Kate, daughter of Michael Balfe, a Catholic landlord in Co. Roscommon; they had no children.

The third son, John, was the only one who had a serious interest in politics and who really applied himself. Educated at Clongowes, as were all O'Connell's sons, and at Trinity College, Dublin, John became a barrister in 1837. As he had been an MP since 1832 and was needed by his father for regular attendance in parliament he had no chance of building up a legal practice. In 1838 he married Elizabeth, daughter of Dr James Ryan, a medical practitioner of Bray, Co Wicklow. MP for various boroughs almost continually from 1832, John retired from political life in 1857 on becoming Clerk of the Hanaper, a government post carrying a salary of £800 a year. When he died in 1858 his funeral was reported by the *Dublin Evening Post* as the largest seen in Dublin since his father's eleven years previously.[18] Immediately after the funeral a committee was established under the chairmanship of the Lord Mayor to organize a national collection in aid of John's eight children who were left inadequately provided for.[19] £5,000 was raised, partly in church and other local collections and partly in donations from prominent Dubliners. The donors included John Gray, the Protestant nationalist and owner-editor of the *Freeman's Journal*, which published an editorial in support of the fund.[20]

Politically John was easily the most important of his father's sons because he played a leading role in the Repeal Association during the last year of his father's life, and he tried, but failed, to keep that Association alive after his father's death. He spoke too often and too long in that body, and he provoked much hostility. The obituaries in the press reflect that hostility where they say they will refrain from dealing with the more controversial aspects of his career, but they tend to agree that he was sincere, able, well-informed and very hardworking. Webb's *Compendium of Irish Biography*, published in 1878, sums him up with the sentence:

> An amiable and conscientious man, he was generally respected but he was quite unable to sustain the role of leader of the Repeal agitation after his father's decease.[21]

Two years later, in 1880, John's bones were dug up by the redoubtable Charles Gavan Duffy. In his semi-autobiographical histories, *Young Ireland* (1880) and *Four Years of Irish History 1845-1849* (1883), Duffy described John as jealous, unscrupulous, narrow-minded and incompetent, as trading on his father's popularity and cajoling the Catholic clergy into opposing the Young Irelanders. Duffy invented the thesis in these books that O'Connell was senile in his last years — a thesis that does not stand up to critical examination — and he used the thesis to accuse John of having induced his allegedly senile father to quarrel with the Young Irelanders and drive them out of the Repeal Association. Duffy's books became the standard history of the Young Ireland period, and consequently John O'Connell's reputation went down for the count. Today, however, Duffy is no longer regarded as a reliable historian, so that John's reputation is due for reappraisal.

In his famous book, *The Fall of Feudalism in Ireland*, Michael Davitt demolished what was left of John's reputation after Gavan Duffy had done with it, in this passage (p. 47):

> It is related that Mr John O'Connell, M.P., eldest [*sic*] son of the

Liberator, read aloud in Conciliation Hall [meeting place of the Repeal Association], Dublin a letter he had received from a Catholic bishop in West Cork, in 1847, in which this sentence occurred, 'The Famine is spreading with fearful rapidity, and scores of persons are dying of starvation and fever, but the tenants are bravely paying their rents'. Whereupon John exclaimed, in proud tones, 'I thank God I live among a people who would rather die of hunger than defraud their landlord of the rent!' It is not, unfortunately, on record that the author of this atrocious statement was forthwith kicked from the hall into the sink of the Liffey.

An examination of the debates of the Repeal Association for the Famine period — September 1845 until the end of the Association in June 1848 — reveals no letter from a West Cork bishop and no statement of John's even remotely resembling the comment attributed to him by Davitt.[22] It is difficult to believe that any reasonable man would have made such an absurd statement, all the more so in John's case because his comments during the Famine on landlord-tenant relations were consistently anti-landlord. One may safely conclude that John almost certainly never made this statement.

O'Connell bought a partnership for his youngest son, Daniel Jr., in a new brewery in Dublin to which he gave his name. The young Dan did not prosper as a brewer, and ended his connection with the firm in 1841. Though MP for Dundalk 1846-47, Waterford City 1847-48 and Tralee 1853-63, he does not seem to have made any mark in politics. In 1863 he left Ireland to become a Commissioner of Income Tax in London. In 1867 he married Ellen Mary, daughter of Ebenezer Foster, member of a private banking family in Cambridge, England. They had ten children.

In 1825 O'Connell's eldest daughter, Ellen, married Christopher Fitz-Simon, a small Catholic landlord but the representative of an ancient family. They had twelve children. In 1823 the Catholic Association was planned at a dinner party in his ancestral home, Glencullen in the Dublin mountains. The house remains in the family, and the table at which the Association was planned is still in the diningroom. According to Fitz-Simon family tradition, Irish was spoken in the glen into the second half of the nineteenth century. Ellen was a good linguist and had some literary talent, publishing a book of poetry in 1863, *Derrynane . . . and other Poems*.

The most remarkable of O'Connell's daughters was his second whom he always called 'Saucy Kate'. She married her kinsman, Charles O'Connell, a small Catholic landlord in Iveragh, and had eight children. She live up to her father's description to the end of her long life. At a tea

party in Mallow in the 1880s a Protestant lady said to her: 'We claim St
Patrick'. Happily unaware that Patrick was a saint by tradition Kate replied
with a sweet smile: 'And which of your Popes canonized him?'

The youngest of the three surviving daughters, Betsey, married
Nicholas Joseph Ffrench, member of a modest Catholic landowning
family in Co. Roscommon. She had six children but was widowed fairly
young. She suffered from a serious emotional disturbance which took the
form of moral scrupulosity, and there was a question about 1848 of
committing her to a mental home. In 1839 she informed her father of her
scruples and he wrote to her two very anxious letters counselling her to
seek and obey directions from her confessor.[23] When William J.
FitzPatrick was about to publish his two volumes of O'Connell's correspondence in 1888, Betsey was embarrassed at his including these two
letters. She withdrew her objection, however, when he headed the letters,
'To his Daughter' and did not mention her name.

Historians have charged O'Connell with nepotism because of the
number of government posts he obtained for his family. The charge is
technically true but unfair. He had four relatives appointed — his son
Morgan and his three sons-in-law. The four salaries (they were not
concurrent because one son-in-law died five years before another was
appointed) totalled £3,200. This sum was less than the remuneration of
the Master of the Rolls, a judgeship O'Connell was offered but refused.
At almost any time after Emancipation the British Government would
gladly have given O'Connell any job he wanted in order to get him out of
politics. Since he had risen to power as a popular leader he might well
have thought it dishonourable to take a well-paid government post, but
there would have been no dishonour in leaving politics to apply himself
exclusively to his practice at the bar. Had he done so, he could have earned
a great income, perhaps treble the amount in state salaries paid to his
relations.

It is also charged that he sought to advance his family by bringing so
many of them into parliament. This group consisted of his four sons, two
sons-in-law, a nephew and a brother-in-law. Several of these relatives had
little interest in politics, and attendance in London for half the year could
be ruinous to any business they might have conducted in Ireland. Until
1911 MPs were not paid any salary. But these relatives were very useful
to O'Connell. As a political leader he had to have men in the House of
Commons whose votes he could command; and he could use his personal
popularity to have his relations elected when he would have had greater
difficulty in procuring the election of others. He decided whether or not
his relatives should stand for parliament in accordance with political
needs; and he moved his sons from one constituency to another like pawns

on a chessboard. In politics O'Connell's relatives were made to serve him, not he them.

Few popular leaders in any land, but particularly in Ireland, have been equipped so well as O'Connell was, by their family and family background. They provided lineage, wealth, success and an intimate knowledge of humble people. His wife, an intelligent and resourceful woman, gave him domestic security and strong moral support. In contrast to all that had gone before were his children, particularly his sons. These young men lacked the ability, and with the possible exception of John, the energy and ambition of their father's and grandfather's generations. They were a drag on their father financially, but then they and their sisters could claim (though they never did) that he had sacrificed their prospects by subordinating his enormously profitable legal practice to politics during the fifteen or twenty years before Emancipation. Perhaps it was as well that he had docile sons. Had they possessed political ideas and ambitions distinct from his they might have made serious trouble for him in his later years.

7

Lawyer and landlord

In folklore Daniel O'Connell is known as the Counsellor. He was given this title by tradition because of his success as an advocate in defending humble people against laws and court prosecutions which they saw as unjust. He was only known as the Liberator late in life, a title bestowed by his political followers. It was his skill as a lawyer which made him widely known, and prepared the ground for his rise to political leadership.

Having pursued his legal studies in London and Dublin he was called to the Irish bar in April 1798. Like most barristers he had little business at first but by 1805 he was achieving distinction. By 1813 he was making nearly £4,000 a year which meant that he was in the front rank of his profession. In the 1820s his earnings reached a peak of £7,000 and averaged nearly £6,000 a year.

As a Catholic O'Connell was prevented by the Penal Laws from being promoted to the Inner Bar, that is, becoming a King's Counsel (KC for short). He estimated that he would have earned an additional thousand pounds a year had the law allowed him this honour; and being a KC would have saved him from a certain amount of drudgery. He felt keenly having to remain a junior barrister.

Living in Dublin and practising at the Four Courts he was a member of the Munster Bar. This involved attending the assizes at Ennis, Limerick, Tralee and Cork for five or six weeks twice a year, in the spring and the late summer. When he was away on circuit he and his wife wrote to each other four or five times a week, and most of what we know of his day-to-day legal practice comes from these letters.

He enjoyed his profession, once telling his wife from the Cork assizes that 'you know how I love the bustle of the courts'.[1] Years later she told him:

> I ought not, darling, regret so much your going circuit for in general the change and bustle of it is of use to you. It completely does away any little *hippishness* [depression] you may have.

He liked to tell his wife of his courtroom triumphs and of the volume of legal business he was doing. In 1811 he wrote from Cork:

> My success this circuit has been great, very great. I have that vanity which makes me think I have made an impression. You will not laugh at me though anybody else would.

On another occasion he wrote from Ennis:

> There is an immense deal of business here and I do believe not only that I have as much as any barrister but more, a great deal more. Indeed this is as usual a famous town for business. There is a most laudable spirit of litigation.

Again, he told his wife:

> All my prisoners have been acquitted. The dock alone has produced me a small fortune. I had the County Court-house this day for near an hour in a roar of laughter at a witness whom I examined, the judge, jury and all the spectators. I have always remarked that nothing advances an Irish barrister more than the talent of ridicule.

A murder case in which he was the defence counsel has found its way into literature. The murder became the theme of Gerald Griffin's novel, *The Collegians*, and later of Dion Boucicault's play, *The Colleen Bawn*, eventually becoming the subject of Julius Benedict's opera, *The Lily of Killarney*. O'Connell's version was more prosaic:

> You will be surprised to hear that I had a client convicted yesterday for a murder for whom I fought a hard battle, and yet I do not feel any the most slight regret at his conviction. It is very unusual with me to be so satisfied, but he is a horrid villain. In the first place he got a creature, a lovely creature of fifteen, to elope with him from her uncle who brought her up an orphan and to rob him of his all, 100 guineas, and in three weeks after he contrived to get her into a boat on the Shannon with his servant, said when he returned to Glin that he left her at Kilrush, then reported she had gone off with a sea captain, and she was not heard of afterwards for near two months when a mutilated carcase floated on shore or rather was thrown, which was identified to be hers from some extremely remarkable teeth. He will be hanged tomorrow unless being a gentleman prevents him.

The murderer was hanged the following day.

But O'Connell was not always so complacent when he lost a capital case:

> Three men were convicted this day for the murder of the Franks family. I am not satisfied with their conviction. I defended them. If they be really guilty twenty hangings would be too good for them. It is a wretched profession when one has the agony of playing for the human life.

Two days later these three brothers Patrick, Maurice and John Cremin were hanged. They protested their innocence to the end.

The most dramatic of all his cases were the Doneraile Conspiracy trials. George Bond Low, a landlord who was also a magistrate, had been murdered near Doneraile, Co. Cork. Twenty men were arrested and charged with conspiracy to murder, and a special commission of two judges were sent to Cork to try them. The defendants were tried in batches, the first lot being found guilty and sentenced to be hanged. A horseman rushed to Derrynane and begged 'the Counsellor' to defend the remaining prisoners. O'Connell's dash through the night, first on horseback and then by carriage, and his arrival during the second trial, are folklore. By a relentless cross-examination he destroyed the credibility of the witnesses for the Crown so that these prisoners and those in the succeeding trials were acquitted. In consequence the death sentence on the first batch was commuted to transportation.

Four years later, in 1833, he sought a free pardon for Daniel John Leary, one of the defendants in the first batch. His letter to the Chief Secretary in Dublin Castle contains much interesting information. He commends Richard Pennefather, one of the two judges, for conducting the trials justly and humanely, but accuses the local magistrates at Doneraile of suppressing evidence in order to obtain a conviction, and he considers they should be dismissed from the magistracy. Finally, in this letter to the Chief Secretary O'Connell charges the Solicitor-General, John Doherty, with having deliberately put Leary into the first batch of prisoners, who were guilty, in order to be sure of obtaining a conviction against Leary, who was innocent.

The letter is important not only as an account of how the Doneraile Conspiracy trials were conducted but for indicating that a conspiracy to murder did exist.

The most famous political trial in which O'Connell figured was that of John Magee in 1813. Magee was the owner and editor of the principal Irish newspaper, the *Dublin Evening Post*. He was tried for a seditious libel on the administration of the Lord Lieutenant, the Duke of Richmond. Though a Protestant, Magee was a protagonist of Catholic Emancipation, and thereby hung the reason for the trial. Robert Peel, the Chief Secretary for Ireland (and later Prime Minister), hoped to cripple the Catholic agitation by silencing the anti-government press in the person of Magee.

Knowing that the packed jury would bring in a verdict of guilty (as they did), O'Connell threw Magee's case to the winds and delivered a stinging indictment of all government in Ireland over the previous twenty years. Nothing like it for sheer audacity had ever come from an Irish Catholic. His speech was printed and distributed throughout the country. It ranks as one of the great courtroom orations of modern times.

Peel was present at the trial and reported to the Lord Lieutenant:

> O'Connell spoke four hours, completely but intentionally abandoning the cause of his client (I have no doubt with his client's consent) taking that opportunity of uttering a libel even more atrocious than that which he proposed to defend, upon the Government and the administration of justice in Ireland. His abuse of the Attorney-General was more scurrilous and vulgar than was ever permitted within the walls of a court of justice. He insulted the jury individually and collectively, accused the Chief Justice of corruption and prejudice against his client, and avowed himself a traitor, if not to Ireland at least to the British Empire.[2]

To a friend Peel wrote:

> I hope the Chief Justice will not allow the Court to be again insulted and made the vehicle for treason, but that he will interrupt his harangue by committing him to Newgate for contempt of court.[3]

When Magee came up for sentencing some months later, the Attorney-General, the virulently anti-Catholic William Saurin, denounced O'Connell for his conduct at the trial. When he had finished, O'Connell rose and declared that it was only out of respect for the court that he would refrain from chastising (horsewhipping) the Attorney-General. The judges were shocked and warned O'Connell of the criminal nature of his statement, whereupon he repeated it but in phrasing sufficiently careful to evade indictment. He then launched another insulting attack on the Attorney-General's conduct and character.

In his brilliant study, *The King of the Beggars*, Seán O'Faoláin pays special attention to O'Connell's handling of the Magee trial, and then he adds:

> Everybody, indeed, who regards gracious living, nobility in thought

and word and behaviour, must read this demagogue with a curl of
distaste . . . Heaven knows, they may well do so, for O'Connell did
a great deal to kill gentle manners in Ireland, to vulgarise and cheapen
us.[4]

But, O'Faoláin maintains, O'Connell had no alternative if he were to
raise a people from their knees.

Peel was not the only man who thought O'Connell had gone too far.
That view was also held by O'Connell's uncle at Derrynane, Muirish an
Chaipin or Maurice of the Cap, known to posterity as Hunting-Cap. He
wrote his nephew a reprimand:

> However averse and hostile the Attorney-General may be to the
> Catholics . . . the high situation he enjoys as first law officer of the
> Crown demands a degree of respect and consideration from the bar
> which should not be lightly forgot or neglected.

After more in the same strain Hunting-Cap delivered his instructions
for the future:

> I have therefore most earnestly to request, and will even add, to insist,
> that you will in future conduct yourself with calmness, temperance
> and moderation towards him, and that you will not suffer yourself to
> be hurried by hate or violence of passions to use any language
> unbecoming the calm and intelligent barrister or the judicious and
> well-bred gentleman.

Hunting-Cap then expressed his disapproval of the way O'Connell had
played to the gallery:

> The flattering power of popular applause has often subdued reason
> and laid people to acts for which they severely suffered but believe
> me, my dear friend, it has ever proved a very perishable commodity.
> No man of solid sense will ever be anxious to look for or obtain it.

This was the aristocratic eighteenth century expressing its disdain, not
so much for the bourgeois nineteenth as for the democracy of the twentieth.

Had O'Connell followed his uncle's orders and behaved like a
gentleman he would probably have gone down in history as that very able
barrister who assisted Lord Fingall, the leader of the Catholic aristocracy,
in an unsuccessful struggle for Emancipation. Instead, the demagogue
drove the Catholic aristocracy — the men of gentle manners —out of
politics, and by organizing the people he served notice on the Catholic

gentry that political leadership must be earned. The Forty-Shilling Free-holders were not the only Catholics to find the chalice of Emancipation laced with vinegar. But Fingall was not soured. On his deathbed in 1836 he asked to have O'Connell informed that the Catholic aristocracy, including himself, had been 'criminally cowardly', and he continued:

> We never understood that we had a nation behind us. O'Connell alone comprehended that properly, and he used his knowledge fitly. It was by him the gates of the Constitution were broken open for us; we owe everything to his rough work, and, to effect further services for Ireland, there must be more of it.[5]

It is surprising to learn that in the early stages of his career nearly all his clients in civil cases — the profitable side of the legal profession — were Protestants. Catholics feared to employ a co-religionist, particularly one so aggressively political. He furnished this information in evidence before a select committee of the House of Lords in 1825:

> The Roman Catholics had a kind of feeling that they were not quite so secure in the courts (I mean this not to apply to judges, but to the entire machinery) as the Protestants. They, the Catholics, did not like to increase the disfavour by having a Catholic advocate; and there are reasons connected with myself of perhaps more animation, I would call it, and others intemperance, which made them particularly desirous to avoid me; so that I got into professional business by my clients being generally and almost exclusively Protestants.

The question immediately arises that if Catholics were afraid to engage him in civil suits, how did he build up his reputation in folklore as the great defence counsel of humble Catholics in criminal cases (his letters to his wife show that he did most of the criminal business on the Munster circuit)? Why were Catholics not afraid to employ him in criminal cases? The answer to this question is indicated in one of the speeches he made in the House of Commons on the Coercion Bill of 1834:

> I have, in the course of my life, defended as Counsel a greater number of the perpetrators of these [agrarian] outrages, than of any other class of offenders; but I never asked a question in cross-examination, an answer to which could bring out a fact or an opinion tending to mitigate the crime. My defence always supposed the prisoner innocent of the charge, but I never attempted to mitigate the atrocity of the crime. I never quitted an assize town at which Whiteboys were tried, without addressing the public publicly, and expressing my

abhorrence of the crime as well as explaining the injurious effects which it occasioned to those who were engaged in its commission.[6]

This declaration can be accepted as true, for he had a hatred of violence, agrarian and political, and he expressed that hatred in private as well as public at every stage of his career. Since he felt so deeply on the subject he must have been able to convince the courts of his sincerity in condemning the crime while absolving his client. Thus judges and other court personnel and juries could see him impartially as a criminal lawyer.

And finally, one must consider what sort of a barrister O'Connell really was, not just how he behaved in great dramas like the Magee trial but how he behaved on normal occasions, and what kind of a legal mind did he have. The historian finds it difficult to answer these questions directly because it is impossible to judge a barrister from newspaper accounts of trials: he must look to contemporary or near-contemporary witnesses. The present writer has found two whose evidence is impressive, one a contemporary barrister, William Henry Curran,[7] a son of the celebrated John Philpot Curran, the other a young observer of the political scene in O'Connell's last years, Daniel Owen Madden.[8] A third witness to whom one turns is J. Roderick O'Flanagan who was called to the Irish bar in 1838. Unfortunately, his *The Bar Life of O'Connell* is too anecdotal, and for his more analytical comments he leans on Madden.

Curran see O'Connell's knowledge of the law in all kinds of court cases as comprehensive but practical rather than scholarly. He and Madden agree that O'Connell was unrivalled as an advocate in all kinds of law but especially in jury cases. They admire his physical and mental energy, his pertinacity and resource; and while allowing for his ingenuity and apparent play-acting they see him as always cautious. They also agree that he had an acute understanding of the Irish mind which he used to brilliant effect in cross-examining witnesses and appealing to juries, and even in playing on a judge's weaknesses.

Two quotations from their publications are worthy of mention. One expresses Curran's opinion of O'Connell's handling of juries:

> Throw him upon any particular class of men, and you would imagine that he must have lived among them all his life, so intuitively does he accommodate his style of arguments to their particular modes of thinking and reasoning.

Madden was too young to have seen O'Connell perform in court but he must have known barristers old enough to have done so, and he did have some legal training. Though he despised O'Connell as a political leader

he admired his skill as a lawyer. In describing O'Connell's conduct when
he had a weak case, he says:

> He acted the part of an indignant lawyer to perfection; caught up his
> brief-bag in a seeming fury, and dashed it against the witness table
> — frowned — muttered fearfully to himself — sat down in a rage,
> with a horrid scowl on his face; bounced up again, in a fit of boiling
> passion, and solemnly protested in the face of heaven against such
> injustice — threw his brief away — swaggered out of the Court House
> — then swaggered back again, and wound up by brow-beating and
> abusing half-a-dozen more witnesses, and without any real grounds
> whatever, finally succeeded in making half the jury refuse to bring
> in a verdict of 'Guilty'.

The passages contains obvious exaggeration but must not be seen as
caricature. When one remembers O'Connell's outrageous conduct in the
Magee trial one can see him behaving in a manner approaching Madden's
colourful description.

After the end of the Cork assizes in September each year O'Connell
used to take a month's holiday in Kerry. He would visit relatives and
friends there, particularly in the peninsula that runs out into the Atlantic
from Killarney. That peninsula is mountainous and weather-beaten tourist
country, the Barony of Iveragh comprising its remote western part.
O'Connell's rich uncle, Hunting-Cap, lived at Derrynane on the south-
west corner of the peninsula while O'Connell's parents lived some twenty
miles north, close to the hamlet that he helped develop into the small town
of Cahirciveen. The O'Connells were the principal family in Iveragh for
some centuries before O'Connell was born in 1775. His family property
and his dreams were centred in that part of the world.

On the death of his father in 1809 he fell in for an estate with a rental
of about £2,000 though this figure fell to less than £1,500 when peace
came after the end of the Napoleonic Wars. On Hunting-Cap's death in
1825 his estate was divided more or less equally between O'Connell and
his two brothers. Thus from 1825 onwards O'Connell had an income from
land of about £4,000 a year.

Extravagant and open-handed he was always in debt. Generous to poor
relations, he was a 'soft touch', lending money too freely and going
security for people who sometimes let him down. His wife feared his
journeys to Iveragh because of the money he would dispense there. He
contributed much to charitable institutions.[9]

Kerry tradition has it that he was a good landlord, easy on his tenants
when times were bad, and never known to evict. His letters and other

evidence support this tradition, but they also show that it is inaccurate: it needs to be qualified.

In 1812 he told his wife:

> The rents are coming in extremely fast without the smallest trouble as the poor people have a most abundant year of it. Indeed at all times my rents are comfortably paid as I would not consent to have any creature put himself under more rent than the land was well worth.

Rents were easy to pay during the Napoleonic Wars, when agricultural produce fetched high prices, but a depression set in afterwards which lasted many years. Matters got worse when a famine hit the country in 1822. O'Connell expressed his concern in a letter to his daughter Kate:

> There is nothing but grief and woe in Kerry. The people starving and the gentry in bitter want. No rents, no money, the fever and famine raging. May the great God be merciful to them all.

Six months later he instructed his land agent to send him up any rents he could collect, but he cautioned him against being severe. By 1825 normal times had returned, and he took a stronger line on collecting his rents, threatening to evict if necessary. Three weeks later, however, he adopted a more lenient tone.

In 1834 Kerry was struck by cholera, and in letters to his agent O'Connell showed the deepest concern. He instructed him to spare no expense: engage a physician to go around the villages and houses; supply poor families with medicines, bread and meat, and with coal and blankets for warmth; and see that special Masses and other public prayers were said to 'avert the Divine Wrath'. His correspondence shows the same solicitude during the Great Famine. In almost daily communication with the Governments Famine Relief Office in Dublin he arranged for the transport of food to Cahirciveen; and he purchased food at his own expense for distribution to his tenants.

In the middle of the Tithe War in 1832 he ordered his agent to evict a certain tenant and that tenant's near relatives if it were true that he had driven cattle for the local Protestant curate, Rev. Francis Chute. The cattle, O'Connell believed, had been distrained by Chute for non-payment of tithes. His action was autocratic since the man's conduct had nothing to do with his tenancy. The proposed eviction, however, would have won popular approval since any man assisting the tithe-collector was regarded as a public enemy. The Iveragh poet, Tomás Ruadh Ó Súilleabháin, wrote a poem about this time which deals with a widow whose cow was distrained for non-payment of tithes by this very curate.[10] The feeling expressed in the poem shows that Ó Súilleabháin would have applauded the eviction of any cattle-driver employed in the collection of tithes.

In his evidence before the Devon Commission in 1845 O'Connell said:

> I make it an invariable rule never to dispossess a tenant, unless he has misconducted himself in some way, such as by running in debt and ruining himself totally with other persons, dissipating his property in that way; or some flagrant crime, so that a man would not wish to have such a person on his property. For the last thirty-eight years I have not dispossessed any one for any other reasons, and very few at all.[11]

The evidence shown in the above-mentioned letters to his agent, and his statement to the Devon Commission, show that O'Connell was prepared to evict, and on occasion, did evict. Yet Kerry tradition has it that he was never known to evict. Can this contradiction be resolved? Probably it can. In Irish tradition the word eviction has a perjorative implication. It usually means the unjust ejectment of a tenant. Ejectment for failure to pay a reasonable rent, when that failure was the tenant's own fault, would not be regarded as an eviction in this special sense. As long as ejectments ordered by O'Connell did not offend local opinion he would not be thought of as an evicting landlord. However, his instructions to his agent concerning the tenant believed guilty of driving distrained cattle, and his evidence before the Devon Commission, prove that his interpretation of the rights and duties of a landlord were more paternalistic than one would expect in a democratic leader.

O'Connell's land agent from 1822 to 1845 was his cousin, John Primrose, Jr., a native of Iveragh. According to local tradition he was a proud man and unpopular with the tenants.[12] In his biography of O'Connell in Irish, Domnaill Ó Súilleabháin, who was well versed in Iveragh tradition, says that the tenants were afraid to complain to O'Connell of his agent's oppressions through fear of incurring the agent's displeasure. Ó Súilleabháin adds, however, that the tenants did not blame O'Connell for his agent's actions.[13] Since O'Connell mixed freely with the people every autumn at patterns (the annual celebration of a parish's patron saint), races and beagling, it is impossible to believe that his tenants would not have made their grievances known to him. That they did make such reports is shown by a letter in which he reproved Primrose on an estate matter and then added that 'all the other tenants would be sure to complain to me privately of your giving preferences according to your interest and would so complain even without any substantial cause'. In spite of Ó Súilleabháin's statement to the contrary, O'Connell must have known what his tenants thought of Primrose, but he may well have seen in an unpopular agent a useful antidote to his own 'softness' and open-handedness. For all his warmth and spontaneity he could be very calculating.

O'Connell's reputation as a landlord came under fire in a series of letters in *The Times* in 1845. It had commissioned one of its journalists, Thomas Campbell Foster, to tour Ireland and write an account of conditions there. He spent three months on his travels, and published his findings in weekly letters in *The Times* as he went along. In these he made adverse criticisms of many landlords, naming O'Connell as probably the worst.[14] He contended that O'Connell charged unjustly high rents, that a great many of his tenants lived in squalor, that he did nothing to improve the farming on his estate, and that he allowed excessive subdivision in order to win an easy popularity. He did not accuse him, however, of being an evicting landlord which was the charge above all others likely to destroy a landlord's reputation in Ireland.

O'Connell reacted with characteristic energy and vituperation, denouncing Foster as the 'gutter commissioner of *The Times*' and as a 'boundless liar'.[15] Stung by these and other epithets, Foster surpassed O'Connell in scurrility, labelling him a political 'imposter' and 'mountbank', and the son of a huckster shopkeeper whose family were of disreputable origin. Needless to say, O'Connell denied or ridiculed most of the charges, and mentioned among other things in his favour that he had allowed many tenants evicted from other estates to settle on his.

As a check on Foster's findings a second representative of *The Times* visited Kerry. He was William Howard Russell who later achieved fame as a war correspondent in the Crimea. He corroborated Foster's account, both men paying particular attention to the squalor in which the tenants lived in the townland of Derrynane Beg, close to O'Connell's home in the townland of Derrynane Mor. Russell reported that Derrynane Beg comprised sixty-two holdings, the rents varying from £7 a year for the largest to two shillings a year for the smallest.[16] When one realizes that there are only six holdings in the townland today, none of them economically viable, one can understand what conditions must have been like in 1845. In his memoirs written about 1890 Russell returned to the subject:

> I believe the tenants of Derrynanebeg were squatters, the evicted refuse of adjoining estates, who flocked to the boggy valley, where they were allowed to run up their hovels of soddened earth and mud, with leave to turn out their lean kine and cultivate patches of potatoes on the hillside, paying as many shillings as the agent could squeeze out of them.[17]

Foster's point that O'Connell allowed his tenants to subdivide their holdings at will in order to achieve an easy popularity ignored the fact that it was very difficult for a landlord to prevent subdivision unless he pursued a policy of eviction as a result of which his tenants would regard him as a tyrant. The accusation of neglect overlooked the fact that a very busy public life and an incurable tendency to live beyond his means meant that O'Connell had neither the time nor the capital for substantial investment in his property.

Foster paid particular attention to Cahirciveen, the hamlet which O'Connell developed into a small town of about one thousand people. Foster wrote of 'the wretched looking town of Cahirciveen, its dirty unpaved streets, and old-hat-mended windows'. O'Connell retorted that he had spent £4,000 on donations and improvements to the town, and had given perpetual leases for sites for the building of houses at almost nominal rents. Since he itemized most of these benefactions it can be taken that he spoke the substantial truth. Had he lied, everybody in his beloved Iveragh would have known that he lied. Furthermore, Cahirciveen tradition has it that he was a generous landlord to the town.[18]

He did have an English defender — the young Quaker, W. E. Forster (to be Chief Secretary for Ireland at the time of Parnell). He came to Ireland in September 1846 to investigate famine conditions for the English Quakers who were about to send a relief expedition. He spent two nights with O'Connell at Derrynane, and wrote home from north Kerry a few days later:

> I have made a great deal of inquiry in all quarters respecting his tenantry, and I am convinced that the impression made by the report in *The Times* is most unfair and untrue. I should say he is decidedly the best landlord in his district, but owing to his having allowed ejected tenants from other properties to squat on his estate at nominal rents, there are, of course, some wretched cabins.[19]

One can say in conclusion that O'Connell was a very popular landlord, but since he employed a land agent disliked by the tenants, that popularity was largely but not fully deserved. Though generous to Cahirciveen, in the development of which he took pride, he neglected his estate as a whole except in times of hardship. For that neglect there were extenuating circumstances in his busy public life and his extravagance. It must be owned, however, that a great many Irish landlords were short of investment capital so that his neglect would not have elicited from Irishmen the harsh judgments passed by English visitors. Taking all factors into account one can say that O'Connell was a reasonably good landlord.

8

Irish Constitutionalism: a tradition?

A dozen years ago I was talking to the distinguished historian, F.S.L. Lyons, and I was shocked to hear him say that there was no constitutional tradition in Irish politics. When I demurred he advised me not to invent something for Irish history in the way that certain English historians had invented the Whig tradition for English history. Of course he meant that there was no *conscious* tradition of constitutionalism in the sense that there *is* a conscious tradition of violence. In modern Ireland the IRA see themselves as heirs to the IRA of the Sinn Féin Revolution, Fenians and Young Irelanders, Tone and the United Irishmen and back even further to those of our forebears who fought Viking and Norman, Tudor and Cromwellian. However unsound this interpretation of history, a conscious tradition of political violence has existed in Ireland since the days of the Young Irelanders.

Being a descendant of Daniel O'Connell I grew up believing that constitutionalism was a conscious tradition. It went against my prejudices to accept Lyons' view, and it took me painful months to accommodate my thinking to his. I went on to ask myself why there is no conscious tradition when so many Irishmen abhor violence today and in regard to Northern Ireland insist that only constitutional methods be used. Why is it that self-interest and expediency are associated with those methods in the past?

In 1966 Professor James C. Beckett described the position in his 'Ireland under the Union', an essay of seminal importance.[1] Having said much of the two national movements, violent and constitutional, he sees the Sinn Féin Revolution as

> a deliberate reaction against the constitutional nationalist movement which, from O'Connell to Redmond, was accused of having betrayed, by its weakness, its folly and its venality, the rights of the Irish nation.

It is with the venality surrounding the origins of constitutionalism that this study deals. For an explanation of that venality we must go back beyond the days of Home Rule, back to the last years of O'Connell, to those last years as portrayed by the nineteenth century historical writer, Charles Gavan Duffy.

As one of the Young Irelanders and as owner and editor of their immensely popular weekly review, *The Nation,* Duffy played an important role in the quarrel between Young Ireland and O'Connell. This quarrel culminated in July 1846 when O'Connell demanded that all members of the Repeal Association must explicitly pledge their allegiance to non-violence and constitutionalism as fundamental principles, the principles on which the association was founded and which it had always professed. The Young Irelanders had no intention of recommending a departure from the use of constitutional methods but they insisted on retaining as a matter of principle the right to use violence should constitutional methods fail.

The two positions — the Young Irelanders' and O'Connell's — were mutually exclusive. O'Connell formulated these principles in a statement known to posterity as the Peace Resolutions.

In his second historical work, *Four Years of Irish History 1845-1848,* Duffy accuses O'Connell of introducing the resolutions, not to safeguard any principles but as a ploy for expelling the Young Irelanders from the Repeal Association. This interpretation has been accepted by most twentieth-century historians, and no historian, barring myself, has seen fit to controvert it. In an article published in 1977 I flatter myself that I have proved O'Connell introduced the Peace Resolutions for the primary and essential purpose of ensuring that the Repeal Association should remain a fundamentally constitutional organization.[2]

Duffy copperfastened his charge of opportunism against O'Connell in regard to the Peace Resolutions by insisting that he was senile in his last years. This assertion was based on an article in the British medical journal, *The Lancet* of 27 November 1847, written by the French doctor who performed an autopsy on O'Connell's brain. He reported that O'Connell had been suffering for some years from *ramollissement* or softening of the brain. This condition can be described in layman's language as senility.

No contemporary noted any mental decline in O'Connell until the last two months of his life, when there was a general collapse. O'Neill Daunt, who had once been his private secretary, met O'Connell six months before his death and more than three months after the issue of the Peace Resolutions, and wrote in his journal:

> This speech as well as his letter to the moral force Repealers of Cork display unimpaired intellectual power. . . . But his physical energies are plainly decaying.[3]

In order to obtain competent medical advice I sent a photocopy of the article in *The Lancet* to Dr Denis Harriman, one of the most distinguished neuropathologists in England. Harriman diagnosed an infiltrative brain tumour which would not necessarily affect the intellect. He expressed the opinion, however, that the best evidence would be O'Connell's letters.[4] These have been collected and published,[5] and they prove that O'Connell was not senile.

In his histories Duffy attributes O'Connell's hostility to the Young Irelanders, on the one hand, to their honesty and their refusal to truckle, and on the other hand, to his greed for power, intolerance of opposition and susceptibility to sycophants. This portrayal of O'Connell would have shocked public opinion had not Duffy also stated that he was senile, and not only senile but in the hands of his scheming son John. Once the charge of senility was propagated it became necessary to prove that John was a conspirator bent on the vilification of Young Ireland.

The question arises: Why was Duffy able to convince academic historians that O'Connell and his son John were not merely in the wrong in their quarrel with Young Ireland but shamefully in the wrong? The answer is complex. The trends of the time favoured Duffy's thesis. All over Europe the last decades of the nineteenth century and the early decades of the twentieth witnessed an increasing respect for violence and an increasing admiration of heroism in its use. The same period saw a corresponding decline in respect for the rule of law. Romantic Nationalism, introduced to Ireland by the Young Irelanders, had permeated Europe by the end of the nineteenth century. It was an ideology with which the utilitarian nationalism of O'Connell could not compete. Add to these considerations the ability and cleverness of Duffy as an historical writer, and you have nearly the whole of the answer. The remaining part — and it is vital — arises from two stories, one told by Duffy and the other by Michael Davitt. This paper will now deal with those two stories.

In two of his books, *Four Years of Irish History 1845-1849* and *My Life in Two Hemispheres*, Duffy relates the following incident:

> A startling confirmation of the public verdict against Mr John O'Connell as the mischief maker came to me by a curious accident. In the session of '54 [*recte* 1853] one night in the House of Commons, Maurice O'Connell [O'Connell's eldest son and heir] crossed the floor and sat down by me. He had long wished, he said, to correct a misapprehension which he believed existed in my mind, that he had been a party to the disastrous quarrel between his father and the Young Irelanders. On the contrary, he had strongly opposed it and never crossed the threshold of Conciliation Hall (the meeting place

of the Repeal Association) after it had happened while his father lived. John had done it all. His own influence with his father had also been undermined in his old age (as I understood by the same person) . . . While I was sitting, immediately after in the tea room with Dr Brady, Member for Leitrim, and Mr. Swift. Member for Sligo, Mr O'Connell came in . . . and repeated in their presence all that he had been saying to me privately . . . and persisted in representing his complete severance in policy from his brother to an extent that was embarrassing. The conversation was fixed in the memory of all of us by the tragic circumstance that Mr O'Connell died that night.[6]

The importance of this incident is obvious. O'Connell and his son John emerge from it as the guilty party in the quarrel with Young Ireland. The witness for the prosecution is their own flesh and blood. What need we of further testimony? And had I not been a descendant of O'Connell I would have accepted this story as incontrovertible evidence, but being a descendant I decided to investigate. I soon found there *was* need for further testimony.

According to the story Maurice O'Connell died that night. His obituary in the London *Globe* of 18 June 1853 contains the passage,

The Hon. Gentleman had been in the House of Commons up to its rising yesterday morning, and during the day complained of illness but before medical aid had arrived he had sunk into a lethargic state which terminated in his death shortly after midnight.

The death certificate gives the cause of death as 'Congestion of the brain — 12 hours'. This information about his illness and death raises the question whether he was mentally competent when speaking to Duffy that day in the House of Commons.

According to the story Maurice disapproved of O'Connell's treatment of the Young Irelanders so strongly that he never again entered Conciliation Hall while his father lived. It will be remembered that the quarrel took place in July 1846, but from the spring of 1846 until O'Connell's death in May 1847 Maurice was in Kerry managing the family estate and organizing famine relief. Local and family tradition has it that O'Connell had dismissed his land agent, so that Maurice's presence in Kerry was a family necessity. This would not rule out the existence of a political motive, but by neglecting to mention the family motive for his absence from Conciliation Hall Maurice was giving a misleading impression. The correspondence between father and son during that time is published[7] and its tone is cordial. It gives no hint that Maurice was displeased with his father's political conduct. Since the family estate was entailed to him he stood in no danger of being disinherited should he irritate his father.

Of Maurice's attitude towards the Young Irelanders before O'Connell's death we have no evidence beyond a remark of Maurice's at a banquet in Cork in June 1845 which the Young Irelander, Denny Lane, considered hostile.[8] In June 1847, the month after the death, Maurice spoke at two meetings of the Repeal Association. At both he expressed hostility to the Young Irelanders and called on voters in the coming general election to vote only for moral-force candidates.[9] When William Smith O'Brien asked permission for the Young Irelanders to take part in O'Connell's funeral procession, Maurice's response was an implied refusal, and was taken to be such by Smith O'Brien.[10]

All this information about Maurice's conduct and about his illness and death leads to the firm conclusion that as evidence concerning the quarrel between O'Connell and Young Ireland Duffy's story is worthless. This does not mean the alleged incident never took place. What it does mean is that Maurice was either lying or, as is more likely, he was mentally incompetent.

And now we come to the despicable John, the evil genius of his father's supposedly senile years. Had Duffy not written his histories and had Davitt not told his story, John would probably be regarded by twentieth-century historians as an intelligent hardworking man whose ambition to succeed his father as the leader of the Repeal Association far outran his abilities. The son of a great leader who wishes to step into his father's shoes is liable to provoke resentment unless he has outstanding ability and an agreeable manner: John had neither. Nevertheless Alfred Webb's *A Compendium of Irish Biography*, published in 1878, has nothing worse to say of John than the passage:

> An amiable and conscientious man, he was generally respected, but he was quite unable to sustain the role of leader of the Repeal agitation after his father's decease.

And then came Duffy's five books in each of which he left John without a leg to stand on: *Young Ireland* in 1880, *Four Years of Irish History 1845-1849* in 1883, *The League of North and South* in 1886, *Thomas Davis: The Memoirs of an Irish Patriot* in 1890, and in 1893, *My Life in Two Hemispheres*.

Whatever shred of reputation was left to John by Duffy was shattered by Michael Davitt in his book, *The Fall of Feudalism in Ireland*, published in 1904. On page 47 Davitt tells the story:

> It is related that Mr John O'Connell, MP . . . read aloud in Conciliation

Hall, Dublin, a letter which he received from a Catholic Bishop in West Cork, in 1847 in which this sentence occurred: 'The famine is spreading with fearful rapidity and scores of persons are dying of starvation and fever, but the tenants are bravely paying their rents.' Whereupon John O'Connell declared, in proud tones, 'I thank God I live among a people who would rather die of hunger than defraud their landlords of the rent.'

Having told this story Davitt makes the comment:

It is not, unfortunately, on record that the author of this atrocious sentiment was forthwith kicked from the hall into the sink of the Liffey. He was not even hissed by his audience; so dead to every sense and right of manhood were the Irish people reduced in those bleak years of hopeless life and of a fetid pestilence of perverted morality.

This story about John O'Connell, widely known since Davitt's *Fall of Feudalism*, is all but required reading for anyone seriously interested in the history of modern Ireland; and a new edition of the book was published in 1970. The story is quoted in full, and with obvious acceptance of its authenticity, by the Irish lawyer and Nobel Peace Prize winner, Mr Sean MacBride, in a recent work.[11]

It can be said at once that this story is hearsay. Davitt gives no authority beyond stating that 'it is related'. A more important consideration arises from the fact that the Repeal Association was dependent on the support of tenant farmers and their near relatives in the towns — shopkeepers, merchants, doctors and lawyers. A powerful part of its membership were the clergy, who were nearly always the sons or otherwise close relatives of tenant farmers. For John to have made so slavishly pro-landlord a statement would be political suicide. There is thus a *prima facie* case against his ever having made it.

An examination of all John's speeches in the Repeal Association during the Famine reveals no letter from a West Cork bishop and no statement of John's even remotely resembling that attributed to him by Davitt. This does not necessarily prove that he did not make such a statement, since press reports of debates in Conciliation Hall may not have been comprehensive or he might have made the alleged statement elsewhere. What is more significant is that all his references to landlord-tenant relations in the Association during the Famine are adversely critical of landlords. There is also the very important consideration that if he had made such a statement the Young Irelanders would surely have known of it. Yet there is no mention of it in the editorials of *The Nation* or in any of Duffy's books. Taking all these factors into account one can safely conclude that John never made the statement attributed to him by Davitt.

In his *Young Ireland* and *Thomas Davis*, Duffy accuses John O'Connell of organizing a conspiracy, into which he drew his father, for the purpose of attacking the Young Irelanders. Duffy places the attack in the late autumn of 1844. I have written an article entitled, 'Young Ireland and the Catholic Clergy in 1844: Political Deceit and Historical Falsehood',[12] in which I believe I have proved that there was no conspiracy and that, though such an attack was made, the O'Connells had nothing to do with it.

It is a constant theme of Duffy's histories that John O'Connell was a political opportunist. Since he put forward no evidence in support of this charge other than conjecture, the charge is difficult to disprove. There is little that a defender of John can get his teeth into. He can point, however, to one important episode in which John showed courage and attachment to principle; it is in connection with the Ecclesiastical Titles Bill in 1851.

This bill is too well known to need much detailed description. It will suffice to say that the restoration of the Catholic hierarchy in England and Wales in 1850 dubbed by its opponents the 'Papal Aggression', provoked an outburst of fear and indignation among Protestants in both Britain and Ireland. In response to this paranoia, which he himself encouraged with a celebrated public letter, the Whig Prime Minister, Lord John Russell, introduced this bill in Parliament. It made it illegal for any person other than an Anglican to claim jurisdiction as archbishop, bishop or dean over any part of Great Britain or Ireland. Section 3 of the bill made liable to confiscation by the State property held by any such person and gave the State the right to administer property held in trust by any such person. Thus much Catholic Church property would be placed at risk.[13] Catholics in both countries saw the bill as a renewal of religious persecution.

Shortly after the introduction of the bill, the Tory Disraeli put down a motion of censure on the Government for not giving adequate relief in taxation to the agricultural interest. His motion was defeated by 14 votes — 281 to 267. Had it passed, the Whig Government would have had to resign. Five Irish Catholic MPs voted with the Government and were immediately denounced by press and public meetings in Ireland. The five included O'Connell's son Maurice and nephew Morgan John O'Connell and their cousin, William T. Fagan. The two O'Connells weathered the storm but Fagan had to resign his seat for Cork City.

The two MPs for Limerick City were John O'Brien and John O'Connell, and they were both absent from the division on Disraeli's motion. A Catholic meeting in Limerick City, presided over by the Mayor and attended by the Bishop, passed the resolution:

That an Irish member who does not oppose Lord John Russell's Government on every question whatsoever . . . forfeits the confidence of the Catholics in this kingdom; and . . . we pledge ourselves never to entrust our representation to anyone who shall thus prove himself an enemy to our religion.[14]

John O'Brien did penance by promising his constituents in a public letter that he would in future oppose all governments 'identified with religious intolerance'.[15] John O'Connell also wrote his constituents a public letter but he took a different line. He said he had deliberately stayed away from the division because he did not want to commit his constituents to a vote in favour of the Government since that was how he probably would have voted. Had Disraeli's motion passed, a general election would return 'a furiously bigoted majority to the new House of Commons and a much more anti-Catholic bill would be enacted'. He would not pledge himself to vote for or against any particular measure in order to put out a ministry but would judge each measure on its merits.[16] In reaction to his letter the Limerick Corporation called on him by a majority of 18 to 12 to resign his seat.[17] He did so, eventually.

In his book, *The League of North and South*, Duffy says:

Two of his [O'Connell's] sons, his nephew and the men they had taken the most pains to impose on the people, voted to maintain Lord John Russell in power at the very crisis of the contest for religious liberty. It afterwards became public [that earnest efforts had been made] to keep Mr John O'Connell from committing this mean action, but utterly in vain. The public indignation at this disclosure was very intense. The Corporation of Limerick . . . promptly censured him; a blow under which he staggered and which brought his mischievous career to a sudden collapse.[18]

Despite what Duffy wrote of the sudden collapse, John lived to fight another day. In December 1853 he was returned for Clonmel, Co. Tipperary with strong clerical backing. Though opposed by Duffy, he was elected without a contest. In his victory speech, John said:

Retired from public life in 1851, because I could not go [along] with the policy of what I feared were injudicious extremes, I am aptly recalled by you at this moment when . . . the old policy of the country [cooperation with the Whigs] is once more recognized as the true means of obtaining reparation, and going on to new achievements.[19]

Long before the Ecclesiastical Titles Bill reached the statute book the Whig Cabinet regretted ever having introduced it, and they withdrew Section 3, that part of the measure relating to property. No one was ever prosecuted under the Act, and in 1871 Gladstone's Liberal Government quietly repealed it.

This study has dealt at length with the Bill in order to show that on a deeply felt popular issue, John O'Connell was no opportunist but had courage and independence of mind.

Since O'Connell wrote the Peace Resolutions and since John O'Connell was their most active proponent in the Repeal Association, the shame attaching to their reputations in regard to Young Ireland sullied those resolutions — the first and most deliberate statement of constitutionalism in Irish history. What constitutionalist in twentieth-century Ireland would want to see his ideals rooted in nineteenth-century opportunism? Rescuing the two reputations from the slur cast by Duffy, and in John's case, from the contempt engendered by Davitt's story, should go far to rescue Irish constitutionalism from its supposed origin in venality.

9

Ireland, Irish-Americans and Negro slavery

Romantic Nationalism is the name given by historians to the new form which nationalism took at the end of the eighteenth century. This new ideology was rooted in the philosophy of Rousseau with its doctrine of the General Will and its emphasis on differences between peoples, and in the new thinking which reflected sentiment, intuition and insight as opposed to the 'cold' rationalism of the Enlightenment. The French Revolution gave flesh and blood to this development by substituting the exciting sovereignty of the nation for the traditional but now unemotional sovereignty of hereditary kings; and by engaging in a series of wars in which through the *levée-en-masse* a people rushed to the defense of *la Patrie*.

The Germans had long envied the cultural and political ascendancy of the French, and now had to undergo conquest and rule by Napoleon. Seeing what power and energy the new ideology gave to the French the Germans felt that they too must adopt it if ever they were to become culturally and politically independent. Though at first holding each nation to be unique and all nations to be equal the Germans soon came to see their own nation as superior and to feel that the unification of Germany was a sacred necessity. Under the impulse of the new thinking, Europeans began to lose interest in the rights of man, in the rights of all men, and to concentrate their attention on the rights of their own nation. The Enlightenment, with its stress on the universal and the general, was giving way to Romantic Nationalism with its emphasis on the unique and the particular.

In Ireland the standard-bearers of Romantic Nationalism were a group of earnest men, mostly in their twenties, and known as the Young Irelanders. They were usually of the professional classes and often journalists, or lawyers with literary tastes. True to the new ideology they were intensely interested in Irish history and politics and in the culture of Ireland past and present. Becoming conscious of the new nationalism in the early 1840s they eagerly joined the Repeal Association, the organization founded and led by the aging politician, Daniel O'Connell. The aim of this organization was to repeal the Act of Union between Great Britain and Ireland and thus gain self-government for the Irish.

Ostensibly the young men and O'Connell were of one mind, but there were fissures under the surface. One difference arose from the fact that the newcomers were almost exclusively interested in Ireland alone whereas O'Connell, though a zealous Catholic, was in many ways a product of the Enlightenment. A Deist as a young man he had drunk of the *philosophes* and the English rationalists, Paine, Godwin and Bentham. The young men had Ireland as their oyster, but O'Connell's interests embraced the Tolpuddle Martyrs, Poles under Tsarist rule, emancipation for British Jews, separation of church and state for France and Spain and even the Papal States, the peasants in India, and Negro slavery. He was concerned with the Negroes in the British Empire until their emancipation in 1833, and thereafter in the United States. It is with the latter subject that this study deals.

O'Connell's uncompromising hostility to American slavery has been recorded by Gilbert Osofsky, Douglas Riach, Revd Neil O'Connell and, in a more general sense, Owen Dudley Edwards.[1] Irish-Americans had founded many branches of the Repeal Association which were sending generous donations to the parent organization in Dublin. It was O'Connell's policy to accept this money, but if it came from slaveholding states or if acceptance could imply any approval of slavery, he would condemn the institution. Occasionally he would go further and accuse Americans of hypocrisy in posing as the champions of liberty while tolerating slavery. In response to requests by several abolitionists to appeal to the Irish in America to refrain from condoning slavery, and instead to support abolition, O'Connell issued an appeal in 1842 and an even stronger one in 1843 but to no avail. As a consequence many branches of the Repeal Association in America closed, and donations to Dublin declined.

There were many reasons why the Irish in America refused to heed O'Connell. They were competing with free Negroes for jobs in the cities, and feared the effect on the labour market if slavery was abolished. There was also the consideration that many of the Abolitionists were anti-Catholic and anti-Irish. Irish Catholics only came to the United States in large numbers from 1830 onwards, the first numerous immigration of non-Protestants in a land where most saw Catholicism as a superstitious and intolerant religion. In this hostile environment the Irish sought acceptance and would never find it if they were to attack established institutions, and, above all, if they were to support the Abolitionists, who were widely regarded as radicals. Even two Irish bishops, Hughes of New

York and O'Connell's old friend, England of Charleston, South Carolina, condemned him publicly for interfering in internal American affairs.

The Young Irelanders were quick to see the injury to the Repeal cause in O'Connell's denunciations of American slavery and the American people. In January 1844 their immensely popular weekly review, *The Nation*, carried an editorial expressing their concern:

> Repeal must not be put into conflict with any party in the States. The men of the Southern states must not have their institutions interfered with, whether right or wrong. Where is our mission to crusade against the faults of our friends? . . . We might as well refuse English contributions because of the horrors of mill-slavery . . . as quarrel with Americans because of their domestic institutions, however we may condemn and once for all protest against them. We received help on Catholic Emancipation from America in 1828 when they held slaves as now, and from England, then a slave-owner, and now a slave-trader.[2]

In its issue of 23 March 1844 *The Nation* published a letter addressed to the Irish in America from James Haughton, the Dublin merchant, Unitarian and Repealer. He referred in the letter to 'the disposition evinced in *The Nation* to accept of aid and sympathy in carrying out measures for Ireland's independence from American slaveholders.' In a postscript he said: 'Mr Haughton sends this letter to the Editor of *The Nation*, and trusts he will give it a place in his widely-read newspaper.' In publishing both letter and postscript *The Nation* commented that, 'A gentleman so respectable and well-intentioned as Mr Haughton is entitled to be heard, and not the less because he differs from us.'

A year later, in March 1845, *The Nation* carried an editorial expressing approval of the American Senate's vote to annex Texas. The projected annexation had been condemned by O'Connell, by anti-slavery groups in Britain and by American Abolitionists because it would have the effect of strengthening the power of slaveholding states. The editorial can be cited as exhibiting indifference on the question of slavery.

A few days later O'Connell spoke in the Repeal Association on the annexation of Texas, condemned President Polk for 'huckstering in human flesh', and added that 'I want no American aid if it comes across the Atlantic stained in Negro blood'. He was taken respectfully to task by Thomas Davis, the much loved leader of the Young Irelanders:

> I don't think it would be quite just towards myself, and towards those who concur with me, if I did not to some extent express my dissent

from the opinion put forward by my illustrious friend in reference to the American slaveholders. I condemn slavery as much as it is possible to condemn it . . . but I am not prepared to condemn the Americans to the extent to which my illustrious friend goes, or silently to hear the amount of censure which he so conscientiously and so consistently with his opinions casts upon them.[3]

A week later *The Nation* stated in an editorial:

Notwithstanding the slavery of the negro, America is liberty's bulwark and Ireland's dearest ally. Ireland laments and condemns the negro slavery which England planted in America. She [Ireland] would exult at its abolition in all the states, as she rejoices at its extinction in so many; but she knows that its abolition, however possible and right, is difficult and dangerous; she remembers that when she sought England's help for emancipation England held slaves — that few nations on earth but hold or have held them; and finally, Ireland knows that she has no Quixotic mission to hunt out and quarrel for (without being able to redress) distant wrongs, when her own sufferings and thraldom require every exertion and every alliance.[4]

On 31 May 1845 *The Nation* carried the editorial, 'Differences in the Association' in which it described several differences of opinion among members of the Repeal Association, one such difference relating to slavery:

Some persons object to receiving the sympathy of American slaveholders, conceiving that he who holds a slave should be an outlaw from free society. Others deny that the offence committed by Athens, Rome, Spain and England — by Solon and Washington — is to be punished thus; they deny that Ireland has a Quixotic mission to redress all the wrongs of humanity, and they assert that our strength needs husbanding, and should not be directed to such remote quarrels; but all condemn slavery — each allows the purity of the other's motive — and all see that the difference is on a minor and external subject.

Two months later, O'Connell's son John had angry words in the Repeal Association with the attorney, Richard Scott, who had been O'Connell's election agent in the famous Clare election of 1828. Scott was not a Young Irelander but he took the same line as did the young men on the harm done to the Repeal cause by constant denunciation of American slavery. He himself reprobated slavery as strongly as any man, but he thought that the Repeal Association should not be made the vehicle for attacks on Americans, especially since Americans even in the slave states wished to end slavery but found it impossible to do so.[5] As a consequence, the next issue of *The Nation* carried the editorial, 'America and Ireland', almost certainly written by Davis,[6] which expressed the belief that 'the country will not read without some feeling of regret the unhappy discussion of last Monday.' The editorial pointed to the difficulty which Americans would face in freeing the slaves:

> They form the mass of the working population from the Chesapeak to Florida. Their emancipators would disappear amongst them were they enfranchised. The wickedness of slavery has made emancipation perilous; for the negro has all the vices, ignorance, and wild impulses of a slave. Yet the system is doomed to perish; it is receding before the example of the northern and western states; it is unknown in the best and will disappear from the worst, unless some element of wrath is intruded.

During the struggle for Emancipation in the 1820s, the editorial continued, the Catholic Association accepted donations from the slaveholding states of the United States without ever raising the question of slavery, and why should not the same conduct be followed now. This was the second occasion on which a comparison was made between the donations from America in the 1820s and in the 1840s, the first being in *The Nation's* editorial of 13 January 1844. The comparison was invalid since in the 1820s slavery still existed in the British Empire so that American slavery was not a major issue in British or Irish eyes. It was only after the British abolished slavery in their empire that anti-slavery groups in the British Isles fixed their gaze on America.

The debate took a new turn when the Young Irelanders seceded from the Repeal Association and formed their own Repeal organization, the Irish Confederation. At the meeting held on 13 January 1847 to inaugurate the new body, James Haughton asked that it should not accept any donations from American slaveowners.[7] His speech on the matter was replied to by one of the Young Irelanders, the eccentric John Kenyon, a parish priest in Co. Tipperary. Kenyon pulled no punches on slavery in the letter he wrote to *The Nation*:

> Hitherto I have assumed slave-holding to be not only a crime, but a crime of the first magnitude. But it was only for the sake of argument.

I am by no means prepared to admit the fact. The Scriptures nowhere formally condemn this crime. The church has never defined it to be such. Priests and bishops maintain communion with slaveholders, unblamed. They have themselves owned slaves. They may own some yet for anything I know to the contrary.[8]

A week later *The Nation* commented on the matter in the column, 'Answers to Correspondents':

We have to say, once and for all, that we will have nothing to do with 'abolition' for the future, either *con* or *pro*. If negro slavery be an evil, then we will join in Father Kenyon's prayer — May God mend it. But we have really so very urgent affairs at home — so much abolition of white slavery to effect if we can . . . that all our exertions will be needed in Ireland. Carolina planters never devoured our substance, nor drove away our sheep and oxen for a spoil. . . . Our enemies are nearer home than Carolina; and we must be permitted to deal with them first. Mr. Kenyon's letter, indeed, was, perhaps, made necessary by Mr. Haughton's public announcement that the Irish Confederation would [*recte* should] receive no slaveholder's money.[9]

The Nation of 20 February carried two letters, one from Haughton and the other from a Cork supporter of the Irish Confederation, Issac S. Varian, taking the journal to task for using the expression, 'If slavery be an evil'. Varian ended his letter with the sentence, 'Alas! that, so soon after the prostration of an O'Connell, those whom we had set up in his place should have been shorn of their glory!'

At the monthly meeting of the Irish Confederation in April 1847 Haughton was in the chair and made an address in which he urged the members not to accept the blood-stained dollars of American slaveholders. Heckled and interrupted he was forced to bring his address to an end. Later in the meeting he and the other joint treasurer presented the financial report, and then he returned to the subject of slavery:

He had left the Repeal Association because liberty of speech was not permitted there to some of his young friends by whom he was then surrounded; and that night he, their chairman, was the only person to whom liberty of speech was denied. (Cries of no, no). He pleaded for liberty and humanity, and they would not hear him.

William Smith O'Brien — the leader of the Young Irelanders now that

Davis was dead — replied to the effect that Haughton had mistaken the feelings of the meeting altogether. Haughton wished to express one opinion, and the meeting wished to express another. To this Haughton replied: 'It is the fact of my having excited your displeasure — (loud cries of no, no) — when speaking on behalf of the American slaves that pains me.'[10]

At this meeting Haughton objected to but failed to prevent the passing of an address to George M. Dallas, the Vice-President of the United States, whom he accused of being a slaveholder. At a meeting of the Confederation's Council some two weeks later it was reported 'that Mr. Haughton after mature consideration, had resolved to resign the [joint] treasurership and withdraw from the Council, in consequence of the Address of the Council to the Vice-President of the United States.'[11] However, he remained an ordinary member of the Confederation.

In a letter to a friend in America six months later, Haughton expressed admiration of the generosity of Americans for their contributions to the relief of the famine-stricken in Ireland, but this very generosity had helped to destroy Irish hostility to American slavery. As a consequence, 'our public men . . . think more of American sympathy, for political purposes, than of the rights of humanity', and Haughton ended his letter with the passage:

> While O'Connell lived he was true to the cause of the slave; there is not now a popular public man who cares a fig about the slave, or who would risk his popularity by standing out manfully against his oppressor; I made the attempt more than once, and I failed. Your bloodstained dollars have been accepted, and the man-stealer may now walk unrebuked amongst us.[12]

I have already referred in this chapter (p. 122) to O'Connell's appeal in 1843 to Irish Americans to support the American Abolitionists. I now propose to describe that appeal and its background.

In August 1843 the Repeal Association received a letter[13] from the Irish Repeal Association of Cincinnati, Ohio. The letter, which enclosed a donation of 113 pounds sterling, was a long one and took O'Connell to task for denouncing American slavery, and in particular, for supporting the Abolitionists. Since there seems to be no copy of the letter extant, except in an obscure Dublin newspaper, and since it has not been published in any historical work, it is appropriate to describe what it says.

The Cincinnati Repealers point out that Ohio is not a slaveholding state and that slavery is forbidden by its constitution. They go on to say that they have no material interest in slavery (not entirely true since Cincinnati had a flourishing trade with the slaveholding south). They admit that slavery is 'an evil of the highest magnitude', but insist that it existed in America before independence and is built into the economy of the slave-holding states. It is unrealistic, they maintain, to expect slaveowners to ruin themselves and their families by agreeing to emancipation without compensation, and equally unrealistic to expect the entire population of the United States to tax themselves heavily in order to pay that compensation. Furthermore, any immediate emancipation would endanger the survival of the Union. The Cincinnati Repealers go on to deny that comparisons with the abolition of slavery in the British West Indies are relevant since Britain herself paid that compensation.

The Abolitionists, the letter continues, have done much more harm than good. They have damaged the efforts of those seeking gradual emancipation. They have sown discord in whole communities and have roused slaves to sedition and violence so that owners sleep 'under the dread of the midnight torch, and all the demoniacal horrors of a servile outbreak.' Furthermore, the Abolitionists are hostile to Catholics: 'The Roman Catholic Church has no bitterer enemy than the Abolitionists of America.'

If slaves are emancipated, what is to be done with them as free men? The letter answers that question:

> The bondage of the Africans has reduced them to a state of degradation, which shocks the habits and sympathies of the whites. . . . Really inferior as a race, slavery has stamped its debasing influences upon the African, and between him and the white almost a century would be required to elevate the character of the one and destroy the antipathies of the other. The very odour of the negro is almost insufferable to the white; and, however humanity may lament it, we make no rash declaration when we say that the two races cannot exist on equal terms under our government and our institutions.

The Cincinnati Repealers then make the assertion that 'the vast majority of slaves in this country are happy and contented with their bondage.' In regard to 'clothing, food, and personal comfort', the slaves are far better off than the half-starved industrial workers in England; and in sickness and old age the former are provided for by their masters whereas the English workers are left to their own devices.

The latter goes on to make the significant point that Abolitionist doctrines teach the Negro that he has 'the right to steal from the people of Ohio, because he has been held in bondage in Kentucky.' Cincinnati was just across the Ohio River from the slave-holding state of Kentucky, and there were hostile feelings between white manual workers, particularly

Irish and Germans, and both free Negroes and fugitive slaves.[14] In 1836 and 1841 Cincinnati had seen anti-Abolitionist and anti-Negro riots.[15] No doubt, the feelings of the Cincinnati Repealers had been exacerbated by these experiences.

In response to the Cincinnati letter O'Connell prepared an address which was adopted by the Repeal Association in Dublin.[16] It begins: 'Gentlemen — We have read with the deepest affliction, not unmixed with some surprise and much indignation, your detailed and anxious vindication of the most hideous crime that has ever stained humanity.' Having made the comment that 'it was not in Ireland that you learned this cruelty', he castigates the Cincinnati Repealers for their 'totally gratuitous assertion' that the Negroes are an inferior race: 'In America you can have no opportunity of seeing the negro educated. . . . How, then, can you judge of the negro race when you see them as despised and condemned by the educated classes, reviled and looked down upon as inferior?' Instead of being esteemed for the many good qualities which they naturally have, they are deprived of education and then 'judged of, not as they would be with proper cultivation, but as they are rendered by cruel and debasing oppression.'

O'Connell then continues: 'We must refer to your declaration that the two races . . . cannot exist on equal terms under your government and your institutions.' He accuses the Cincinnati Repealers of having 'borrowed the far greater part of your address from the cant phraseology which the West Indian slaveowners, and especially those of Jamaica, made use of before emancipation.' They used to assert 'as *you* do now' that freeing the slaves would mean the massacre of their former owners and their families:

> The emancipation [in Jamaica] *has* taken place. . . . Was there one single murder consequent on the emancipation? Was there one riot, one tumult, even one assault? Was there any property spoiled or laid waste? . . . [On the contrary] the most perfect tranquility has followed the emancipation. The criminal courts are almost unemployed. Nine-tenths of the gaols are empty and open; universal tranquility reigns, although the landed proprietors have made use of the harshest land-lord power to exact the hardest terms, by way of rent, from the negro, and have also endeavoured to extort from him the largest possible quantity of labour for the smallest wages.

And then O'Connell drives home his point,

> The two races exist together upon equal terms under the Briish government and under British institutions. Or shall you say that the

British government and British institutions are preferable to yours? The vain and vapouring spirit of mistaken republicanism will not permit you to avow the British superiority. You are bound, however reluctantly, to admit that superiority, or else to admit the falsity of your own assertions.

Even if the slaveowners would suffer by losing their slaves, a far greater number of persons would receive the boon of liberty, and thus 'the noble Benthamite maxim, of doing the greatest possible good for the greatest possible number, would be amply carried out into effect.'

O'Connell then states that 'every Catholic knows how distinctly slave holding, and especially slave trading, is condemned by the Church.' (Here he was mistaken. The Church had not condemned slavery itself: in 1839 the Pope had condemned only the slave trade.) He berates the Cincinnati Irish for not denouncing what the Pope had denounced, (as O'Connell puts it) 'the diabolical raising of slaves for sale, and selling them to other states.' The sacred principles of Christianity 'have already banished domestic bondage from civilised Europe, and . . . will also, in God's own good time, banish it from America, despite the advocacy of such puny disclaimers as *you* are.'

In Ireland, O'Connell continues, the opponents of Catholic Emancipation expressed their hatred of Catholics by abusing their leaders just as the Cincinnati Irish are expressing their 'bad feelings about the negroes' by abusing the Abolitionists, whom he describes as 'the tried friends of humanity.' He admits that there are among the Abolitionists 'many wicked and calumniating enemies of Catholicity and the Irish', but he advises that the best way of disarming their malice is '*not* by giving up to *them* the side of humanity while you yourselves take the side of slavery; but . . . by surpassing them in zeal for the freedom of all mankind.' He ends his address with the plea: 'Irishmen, I call on you to join in crushing slavery, and in giving liberty to every man, of every caste, creed and colour.'

And now to return to the subject with which this study started, Romantic Nationalism! Given their belief in this ideology the Young Irelanders were merely being logical. Irish nationalism was the cause to which they were dedicated, and they had little interest in the welfare of peoples in other lands. Their repeated condemnations of slavery need not be taken too seriously. Those condemnations were merely a preface to their demand that O'Connell stop condemning slavery because he was damaging American support for Repeal. Had they neglected to condemn slavery they would have handed O'Connell an important debating point. When several of the leading Young Irelanders settled as exiles in America they kept clear of the subject except for two of their number, John Mitchel and Thomas

Francis Meagher, who publicly defended slavery. In his study of American opinion on Ireland Owen Dudley Edwards has written: 'O'Connell did his country better service than Young Ireland was to do. Indeed the record of Young Ireland on the slavery issue reinforces one's conviction that the image of Ireland in America was greatly enhanced by O'Connell's memory where otherwise it would have suffered.'[17]

To be fair to the Young Irelanders it must be said that O'Connell was far from being an ordinary Catholic. His approach to slavery was rooted in the universality and humanitarianism of the Enlightenment, enriched by a lively Catholic faith. Paradoxically, this Child of the Enlightenment was in his maturity a Catholic polemicist and *religieux*. In discussing O'Connell's social and economic outlook Professor Joseph Lee has written:

> Catholic social teaching consisted of little more than commending charity and preaching the integrity of the family. . . . O'Connell then felt intense commitment to his version of Catholic social teaching. His Benthamism was essentially ethical rather than doctrinal. . . . Why he chose to interpret Catholic doctrine in this particular manner raises interesting issues, which remind us just how little we know about the religion of this remarkably religious man.[18]

10

Daniel O'Connell, 1775-1847

Born: 6 August 1775; near Cahirciveen, Co. Kerry, Ireland
Died: 15 May 15 1847; Genoa, Italy
Area of Achievement: Law, government, politics, and social reform
Contribution: Once the leader of the struggle for Catholic emancipation in the British Empire, O'Connell is identified with the principles of religious freedom and separation of church and state, non-violent reform movements, early democratic organizations and the upholding of the rule of law.

Early Life
Daniel O'Connell was born on 6 August 1775, on the southwest coast of Ireland near the small town of Cahirciveen (then a hamlet), in the barony of Iveragh and county of Kerry. Iveragh is situated at the western end of a mountainous peninsula running forty miles out into the Atlantic from the Lakes of Killarney. Its mountains and sea inlets afford beautiful scenery, and nowhere more so than at Derrynane, where O'Connell's family lived from the beginning of the eighteenth century (Derrynane is now preserved as a national monument). Iveragh had retained much of the Gaelic culture so that O'Connell was born into a society in which perhaps a majority of the people knew no English. Catholic landlords, the O'Connells were the principal family in Iveragh for some centuries before O'Connell was born in 1775. Fostered out at birth to a tenant of his father, in accordance with Gaelic custom, he returned to his parents' house at the age of four knowing no English. He was the eldest son in a family of ten children. His father ran a general store in Cahirciveen and invested his profits in the purchase of land. His mother was a daughter of John O'Mullane, a Catholic small landlord of old family in County Cork. When still a boy, O'Connell was adopted as heir by his rich but childless uncle at Derrynane. Receiving his first schooling at Derrynane, he then proceeded to a boarding school near the city of Cork. In 1791, he was sent to France, first to the college of St Omer and then to the English college at Douai. In January 1793, Douai

was closed by the French revolutionary government, and O'Connell left for England as virtually a refugee, a day or two after the execution of Louis XVI. He spent the next three years as a law student in London and then obtained his uncle's permission to complete his legal studies in Dublin, where he was called to the bar in 1798.

Moderately tall and broadly built, O'Connell looked impressive and distinguished rather than handsome, though his expressive blue eyes were commented upon. Having a powerful voice, he was one of the famous orators of his day, being able to appeal to more educated audiences as well as to great crowds. Although actively engaged in politics, he built up one of the largest practices of his day at the Irish bar. Because of his skill in defending great numbers of poor Catholics against charges they considered unjust, he early won widespread popular fame.

In 1802, O'Connell married his distant cousin, Mary O'Connell, one of the eleven penniless children of a Co. Kerry physician. For this impecunious marriage, he was disinherited by his uncle. Three years later however, uncle and nephew were reconciled, and eventually O'Connell was bequeathed Derrynane and a third of his uncle's estate. The marriage was a very happy one, the only cause of distress being his extravagance, which left him always in debt. The charge that he was a womanizer is not supported by historical evidence. That it has been made can be explained by the fact that he was the last of the Gaelic folk heroes, and all these heroes from prehistory onward had a reputation for sexual energy — it was seen as part of their greatness — and O'Connell was no exception.

O'Connell entered politics in 1800, when he organized a meeting of Dublin Catholics to oppose the enactment of the Union between Great Britain and Ireland (whereby the Irish Parliament was abolished, and Ireland for the future elected representatives to the British Parliament). He seems to have been the only member of the Catholic propertied classes to oppose the Union. By 1805, he was an energetic member of the Catholic Committee, a body of landlords, businessmen, and lawyers who sought full freedom and equality for Catholics so that they could enter Parliament and government service and not remain a subject people.

Life's Work
Politics in Great Britain and Ireland was at that time a matter for landlords and members of the upper-middle class, for aristocratic dinner parties and to a lesser extent for committees and small public meetings. O'Connell was to alter this pattern when he founded the Catholic Association in 1823, which proved to be the first great popular democratic organization. In February 1824, he introduced the penny-a-month plan, whereby tens of thousands of the poorer classes were enrolled and politically instructed.

By the end of 1824, the whole country was roused, and for the next four years the Catholic Association exerted strong pressure on the British government. In 1828, there occurred a by-election for Co. Clare, and O'Connell was induced to contest it, the first Catholic to stand for Parliament since the seventeenth century.

It was realized from the start that the Clare election would be decisive. The contest was bitter, and O'Connell, who could be scurrilous, left nothing unsaid or undone to ensure victory. Special contingents of army and police stood by to deal with popular violence, but there was none. Instead, as great numbers gathered in and around the county town of Ennis, where the polling took place, the officials of the Catholic Association with the assistance of the clergy imposed strict discipline, even to the extent of banning the consumption of liquor. On the fifth day of the polling, when the count was two-to-one in O'Connell's favour, the Tory candidate conceded victory. Organized, disciplined, and instructed, the masses had shown their power. In the weeks that followed, the two chief members of the Tory cabinet, the Duke of Wellington as prime minister and Sir Robert Peel as home secretary (the minister in charge of Ireland), decided that Catholic emancipation must be enacted. Accordingly, in the spring of 1829, Peel introduced the bill which was passed by both houses without difficulty and received the royal assent in April.

The reasons for which the anti-Catholic Tory government conceded emancipation have frequently been misunderstood. The threat of civil war in Ireland is usually given as the reason, but that factor would not have been sufficient if the British body politic were united in defence of the Protestant establishment in Ireland. There was no such unity. The Whigs and their Radical supporters, who together made up nearly half of the House of Commons, were sick of the long agitation for emancipation. Though not necessarily committed to any principle of religious freedom, they did respond to the Whig tradition of government by consent. Also, some of the more liberal of the Tories were prepared to concede. Should the Tory administration, by rejecting emancipation, provoke a civil war in Ireland, they might find themselves voted out of office and replaced by a Whig government willing to enact the measure. There was the additional consideration that twenty or thirty Catholics might be returned for Irish constituencies at the next general election, and the Mother of Parliaments could look ridiculous if she refused them admission. In demanding emancipation for Catholics, O'Connell was careful to ask for it only on the general principle of freedom and equality for men of all religions. As early as 1807, he rested his case 'on the new score of justice — of that justice which will emancipate the Protestant in Spain and Portugal, the Christian in Constantinople.'

Once elected to Parliament, he applied his energies to a large number of causes. These included the extension of the parliamentary and local government suffrages; the Tolpuddle Martyrs; Poles persecuted by czarist Russia; Jewish emancipation; separation of church and state in Catholic as well as in Protestant countries, and even in the Papal States; free trade and especially the repeal of the Corn Laws; and the abolition of black slavery. In pursuing these aims, he was the leading Radical in the British Parliament in the 1830s.

With the passing of the Emancipation Bill, O'Connell hoped for great things for Irish Catholics, but his hopes were only partly realized. The Tories and the more conservative of the Whigs were determined to maintain Protestant dominance in Ireland and not to admit Catholics to office. In the general election of 1834, however, the Whigs lost their overall majority and were forced to come to terms with O'Connell if they wished to maintain a stable government. They negotiated an arrangement whereby O'Connell's party of some twenty-five Members of Parliament would support the Whigs and keep them in power provided they admitted Catholics to the Irish administration and sponsored certain reforms. As a consequence, the Protestant monopoly of power was broken, and Catholics were appointed to the civil service, the judiciary, and high posts in a modernized and expanded police force. The legislative reforms demanded by O'Connell were passed by the Commons but amended in an anti-Catholic direction by the House of Lords. Nevertheless, gains were made.

When the Tories returned to power in 1841 with a large majority in the House of Commons, O'Connell believed that he could look for no further reforms. When his year as lord mayor of Dublin ended in October 1842, he threw himself into the struggle for Repeal, that is, the repeal of the Act of Union. British political opinion was determined to uphold the Union, seeing Repeal as involving sooner or later the breaking away of Ireland from the Empire. It was also considered that control of Ireland was essential to British military security. The question the historian must ask is: How could a perceptive politician such as O'Connell, with a long experience of British politics, believe that he could win Repeal? The only answer that makes sense is that he knew he could not; he was using the carrot of Repeal to rouse the Catholic masses so that, as in the case of Catholic Emancipation, he could intimidate a British government into granting not Repeal but major reforms. Whatever his purpose, he had the Repeal Association hold great public gatherings known as monster meetings throughout the country, at which he made menacing speeches. Peel's nerve held, however, and in October of 1843, he called O'Connell's bluff by proclaiming the monster meeting announced for Clontarf outside

Dublin. O'Connell called off the meeting.

Peel, however, was not the proverbial Bourbon. He realized that the Repeal movement was a response to real grievances, and in the years left to him as prime minister he enacted several reforms pleasing to the Catholic clergy and middle-class Catholics in general, and he planned to enact a measure giving tenant farmers a degree of legal security. Unfortunately for Irish Catholics, Peel was driven from office in 1846 by the Whigs (aided by O'Connell) and a majority of his own Tory Party, as soon as he had enacted the repeal of the Corn Laws.

The Repeal movement brought to the fore a group of idealistic young men who soon came to be known as the Young Irelanders. On the declared policy of Repeal, they were ostensibly at one with O'Connell, but there were fissures under the surface. Where he drew his political principles from the *philosophes* (excluding Jean-Jacques Rousseau) and the English Rationalists, Thomas Paine, William Godwin, and Jeremy Bentham (though a zealous Catholic in his maturity O'Connell had been a Deist as a young man), the Young Irelanders subscribed to Romantic Nationalism, the ideology then sweeping through Europe. O'Connell saw the nation as a collective unit, as the sum of all of its parts, whereas the young men realized that a nation is first and foremost a tradition; from that reality, they drew conclusions that bore little practical relevance to their own day but which would inspire later generations.

Unrealistic in the context of contemporary politics, the Young Irelanders demanded that the small Repeal Party should act independently of the Whig and Tory parties in the British Parliament and that O'Connell must not renew his 'alliance' with the Whigs; they rightly suspected that, contrary to his declared policies, he intended to do just that. Though he tolerated much public criticism from the Young Irelanders, he often acted as if the Repeal Association were his private property and as if he were not bound by its decisions. The break between old and young came in July 1846, on the question of violence. O'Connell insisted that all members of the Repeal Association must adhere to the principles of non-violence and constitutionalism, on which the association had been founded and to which the members had pledged their allegiance repeatedly since then. The Young Irelanders insisted that these alleged principles were merely policies. They were constitutionalists by preference, but they considered that the use of violence might be necessary at some time in the future should constitutional methods fail. The two positions were mutually exclusive. The majority of the population sided with O'Connell, regardless of whether they understood the points at issue, but it was his last victory. Within months, the famine was ravaging the country, and by February 1847, O'Connell knew himself to be dying. On the advice of his doctors, he set out on a pilgrimage to Rome but died on the way at Genoa on 15 May 1847.

Summary
Daniel O'Connell deserved the title 'the Liberator', which was bestowed on him by his followers after Catholic Emancipation. Though he had able Catholic lieutenants and received valuable cooperation from a number of Irish Protestants, he was the central figure in politically instructing and organizing a subject people. Catholic Emancipation was the first political victory they knew after two centuries of discouragement and failure, and it was irreversible. The Catholic Association was the first popular democratic organization of the modern world. O'Connell was the first Catholic political leader and perhaps the first politician in any major Christian denomination in Europe to espouse the dual principles of religious freedom and separation of church and state. In the years from Catholic Emancipation until his death, he was the outstanding European opponent of Black slavery. As a practitioner of non-violent reform, he ranks with Mahatma Gandhi and Martin Luther King. He embraced and expanded the British Whig tradition of government by consent which owed much to another Irishman, Edmund Burke. Future generations may well recognize him as the greatest upholder of the rule of law — not merely of law as made by one's own people but also of law as made by others — that Western civilization has produced.

Notes

Chapter One: *Income and expenditure*

1. Mary O'Connell was the daughter of 'mixed' marriage, her father a Protestant (estalished church), her mother a Catholic. Her paternal grandfather, Maurice O'Connell of Emlaghmore, Waterville, Co. Kerry, had become a Protestant in 1730. In accordance with the custom of the time she and her sisters were reared as Catholics, her brothers as Protestants. On first consideration it might seem that Hunting-Cap's hostility to the marriage was prompted by the thought that Mary's branch of the O'Connell family had behaved dishonourably in becoming Protestant, but there is no evidence whatever to support this view. The lack of a dowry was unquestionably the vital consideration. This conclusion is strengthened by much evidence throughout O'Connell's correspondence of the importance attached by his relatives and even by himself to dowries. In 1825, after twenty-three years of married life and having borne eleven children, Mary was still sensitive of having brought her husband no dowry.
2. Mary O'Connell to O'Connell, 18 or 19 Nov. 1803 (N.L.I., O'Connell papers, herereafter cited as O'C. P.).
3. Mary O'Connell to O'Connell, 14 Dec. 1803 (O'C. P.).
4. Mary O'Connell to O'Connell, 12 Aug. 1805 (O'C. P.).
5. This information is contained in a document entitled 'Copy of a case on behalf of Daniel O'Connell [grandson of O'Connell] for the advice and opinion of Abraham Brewster, Q.C.' in the O'Connell MSS in University College, Dublin.
6. O'Connell to Mary O'Connell, 31 Mar. 1806 (Papers of Lt-Col. M. O'Connell Fitz-Simon, M.C., Glencullen House, Co. Dublin, hereafter cited as F.-S. P.).
7. O'Connell to Mary O'Connell, 13 Oct. 1809, 2 Apr., 20 Aug., 5, 30 Sept., 8, 14 Oct. 1810 (F-.S. P.).
8. Based on a list of townland rents in the Fitz-Simon Papers.
9. James O'Connell to O'Connell, 26 Oct. 1811 (University College, Dublin, O'Connell MSS, hereafter cited as O'C. MSS). The figures actually given by James O'Connell are for a half year. They have been doubled to produce the figures stated in the text.
10. Count O'Connell to O'Connell, 30 July 1819 (F.-S. P.).
11. James O'Connell to O'Connell, 19 Nov. 1823 (O'C. P.).
12. 'Copy of a case on behalf of Daniel O'Connell' (as above).
13. Ibid.
14. Maurice O'Connell to Pierce Mahony, 11 Nov. 1848 (Papers of Lt-Col. and Mrs R. K. Page, Rathcon, Grangecon, Co. Wicklow, hereafter cited as Rathcon Papers).

15. *Correspondence of Daniel O'Connell*, ed W. J. Fitzpatrick (London, 1888), I, p. 26.
16. O'Connell to Mary O'Connell, 1 Aug. 1814; 9, 12 Mar., 12, 18 July, 1815; 21 Mar., 30 July, 14, 22 Aug. 1816; 12 Mar. 1817 (F.-S. P.).
17. James A. Reynolds, *The Catholic Emancipation Crisis in Ireland 1823-1829* (Harvard University Press, 1954), p. 38n.
18. M. J. O'Connell, *Last Colonel of the Irish Brigade* (London, 1892), II, p. 272.
19. Hunting-Cap to O'Connell, 15 Feb. 1798 (O'C. P.).
20. O'Connell to Denis McCarthy, 20 Jan 1806 (N.L.I., MS 5759).
21. O'Connell to Mary O'Connell, 31 Mar. 1806 (F.-S. P.).
22. Mary O'Connell to O'Connell, 2 Apr. 1806 (O'C. MSS).
23. Splinter was the nickname of another Daniel O'Connell, an attorney in Tralee. He was a distant cousin as well as a brother-in-law of O'Connell and was disapproved of by O'Connell's family.
24. Mary O'Connell to O'Connell, 31 Mar. 1808 (O'C. P.).
25. Mary O'Connell to O'Connell, 18 or 25 Sept. 1809 (O'C. P.).
26 Hunting-Cap to O'Connell, 16 May 1811 (F.-S. P.).
27. The existence of this promise can be inferred from Mary's letter to her husband of 14 March 1815 (O'C. P.).
28. O'Connell to Mary O'Connell, 13 Mar. 1815 (F.-S. P.).
29. Mary O'Connell to O'Connell, 14 Mar. 1815 (O'C. P.).
30. Mary O'Connell to O'Connell, 9 Aug. 1816 (O'C. P.).
31. James O'Connell to O'Connell, 4 Jan. 1816 (O'C. MSS).
32. Ibid.
33. James O'Connell to O'Connell, 17 Feb. 1816 (O'C. MSS).
34. O'Connell to Mary O'Connell, 21 Mar. 1816 (F.-S. P.)
35. James O'Connell to O'Connell, 1 Mar. 1817; 13 Jan. 1826 (O'C. MSS).
36. James O'Connell to O'Connell, 1 Mar. 1817 (O'C. MSS).
37. James O'Connell to O'Connell, 28 Dec. 1821; 13 Jan. 1826 (O'C. MSS).
38. O'Connell to Mary O'Connell, 8 Apr. 1822 (F.-S. P.).
39. O'Connell to Mary O'Connell, 5 Apr. 1822 (F.-S. P.).
40. O'Connell to Mary O'Connell, 8 Apr. 1822 (F.-S. P.).
41. James O'Connell to O'Connell, 17 Feb.; 28 Mar. 1822 (O'C. MSS).
42. O'Connell to Mary O'Connell, 11, 12 Mar.; 3, 4, 11 Apr.; 3, 15 May 1822 (F.-S. P.)
43. O'Connell to Mary O'Connell, 4 May 1822 (F.-S. P.).
44. O'Connell to Mary O'Connell, 18 May 1822 (F.-S. P.).
45. Mary O'Connell to O'Connell, 26 May 1822 (O'C. P.).
46. James O'Connell to O'Connell, 28 Mar. 1822 (O'C. MSS).
47. James O'Connell to O'Connell, 8 Sept. 1823 (O'C. MSS).
48. James O'Connell to O'Connell, 11 Sept. 1823 (O'C. MSS).
49. James O'Connell to O'Connell, 16 Sept. 1823 (O'C. MSS).
50. James O'Connell to O'Connell, 3 Nov. 1823 (O'C. MSS).
51. Rev. Peter Kenney, S.J., to O'Connell, 6 Nov. 1823 (O'C. MSS).
52. Denys Scully to O'Connell, 23 Nov. 1823 (O'C. P.).
53. Mary O'Connell to O'Connell, 4 Feb. 1824 (O'C. P.).
54. Ibid.
55. Mary O'Connell to O'Connell, 10 Feb. 1824 (O'C. P.).
56. O'Connell to Mary O'Connell, 16 Feb. 1824 (F.-S. P.).
57. Mary O'Connell to O'Connell, 10 Feb. 1824 (O'C. P.).
58. Mary O'Connell to O'Connell, 27 Feb. 1824 (O'C. P.)
59. O'Connell to Mary O'Connell, 22 Jan. 1823 (F.-S. P.).

60. This information is contained in a statement of Hunting-Cap's assets, apart from land, signed by John Primrose, Jr., O'Connell's land agent (O'C. MSS).
61. James O'Connell to O'Connell, 27 Jan. 1825 (O'C. MSS).
62. This information is contained in the statement of Hunting-Cap's assets (ibid.).
63. James O'Connell to O'Connell, 27 Jan. 1825 (O'C. MSS).
64. James O'Connell to O'Connell, 9 Apr. 1825 (O'C. MSS).
65. In 1818 O'Connell calculated that his income from land after Hunting-Cap's death would be £4,000 a year (O'Conneil to Mary O'Connell, 26 Mar. 1818, F.-S. P.). This estimate is supported by Count O'Connell's letter to O'Connell of 20 Mar. 1825 (F.-S. P.).
66. O'Connell to A. V. Kirwan, 8 Nov. 1837 (*Corr. of O'Connell*, II, pp 117-19)
67. Count O'Connell to O'Connell, postmarked 10 Feb. 1826 (F.-S. P.).
68. Ibid.
69. James O'Connell to O'Connell, 23 Sept. 1826 (O'C. MSS).
70. Count O'Connell to O'Connell, 30 July 1819 (F.-S. P.).
71. James O'Connell to O'Connell, 19 May 1827 (O'C. MSS).
72. Ibid.
73. A book-keeping account of the payment is in the Fitz-Simon Papers.
74. O'Connell to Mary O'Connell, 21 June 1827 (F.-S. P.): O'Connell to John Primrose, Jr., 5 Aug. 1827 (O'C. MSS).
75. O'Connell to John Primrose, Jr., 14 June 1825 (Papers of Mrs Maurice Quinlan and Miss Katie Fitzgerald, Kenneigh House, Aghatubrid, Co. Kerry).
76. O'Connell to Mary O'Connell, 1 Dec. 1827 (F.-S. P.).
77. O'Connell to Mary O'Connell, 4 Dec. 1827 (F.-S. P.).
78. Reynolds, *Emancipation Crisis*, p. 38n.
79. O'Connell to Mary O'Connell, 3 Apr. 1822 (N.L.I., MS 5759).
80. O'Connell to Mary O'Connell, 31 May 1822 (F.-S. P.).
81. O'Connell to Mary O'Connell, 5 June 1822 (F.-S.P.).
82. Mary O'Connell to O'Connell, 13 Sept. 1819 (O'C. P.).
83. Mary O'Connell to O'Connell 1 Dec. 1825 (O'C. P.).
84. James O'Connell to O'Connell, 28 Mar. 1822 (O'C. MSS).
85. Information in a letter of 8 January 1969 from Rev. Mother, Presentation Convent, Cahirciveen, Co. Kerry, to the author.
86. J. D. FitzPatrick, *Edmund Rice* (Dublin, 1945), p. 266.
87. This figure is calculated on a *hurried* examination of the lists of subscriptions in the *Freeman's Journal*, Apr.-Dec. 1829.
88. O'Connell to P. V. Fitzpatrick, 12 May 1846 (*Corr. of O'Connell*, II, pp. 373-5).
89. James O'Connell to O'Connell, 18 Dec. 1837 (O'C. MSS): Maurice O'Connell to Pierce Mahony, 24 Dec. 1848 (Rathcon Papers).
90. O'Connell to Christopher Fitz-Simon, 13 Sept. 1826 (F.-S. P.): James O'Connell to O'Connell, 23 Sept. 1826 (O'C. MSS): Morgan O'Connell to O'Connell, 21 May 1846 (O'C. P.).
91. This quotation and subsequent information are taken from the certified copy of O'Connell's will in the O'Connell MSS.
92. Most of the information on O'Connell's financial affairs after his death has been found in the letters written to Pierce Mahony in the Rathcon Papers. That funds were not sufficient to pay the whole of the £8,000, or even the greater part of it, is suggested in particular by the letters to Pierce Mahony from O'Connell's son John of 13 and 16 Dec. 1848 and 9 Mar. 1849.
93. After his father's death Maurice O'Connell bought a yacht for £1,260 (Daniel Leahy

to Pierce Mahony, 11 Oct. 1848: Maurice O'Connell to Pierce Mahony, 10 Dec. 1848, Rathcon Papers). Mahony insisted that the yacht must be sold and Maurice agreed to sell it (Maurice O'Connell to Pierce Mahony, 19 Dec. 1848 and 4 Apr. 1849, Rathcon Papers). In one of his letters Maurice said wistfully, 'I am ready therefore to do as you and my other friends point out. I have been too long trained to suppress and sacrifice my own feelings, in order to give way to my dear father's wishes and orders, to suffer much from any struggle against them at present' (Maurice O'Connell to Pierce Mahony, 17 Dec. 1848, Rathcon Papers). In defending his purchase of the yacht, Maurice wrote: 'There is nothing men are more intolerant in than in their ideas of matters of amusement, and they do not see why all men should not be pleased with their own peculiar recreations. It was the only weak point in the Liberator's character. His only touch of *bigotry* was as a *hare hunter*' (Maurice O'Connell to Pierce Mahony, 25 Dec. 1848, Rathcon Papers).

94   The furniture in the house in Merrion Square was sold in September 1847 (*Freeman's Journal*, 11 Sept. 1847). The books were sold in a six-day auction in May 1849 for disappointing prices (*Freeman's Journal*, 23, 24, 25, 26, 28 and 29 May 1849). It is a rather vague tradition in the O'Connell family that most of the furniture in Derrynane was also sold.

Chapter Two: *Religious freedom*

1. In the late nineteenth and twentieth centuries it has been possible for religious freedom to exist where there is an established church but only where that church has been shorn of its substantial privileges. But such conditions did not prevail until the second half of the nineteenth century.

2. By a major Christian denomination I mean one sufficiently numerous and powerful in its membership to become an established church in at least one European state, for example, Roman Catholics, Anglicans, Lutherans, Presbyterians, Orthodox Catholics.

3. In 1787, 1789, and 1790 Charles James Fox stated in the House of Commons that no man should suffer any political discrimination on account of his religious beliefs, but he made it clear that he was not giving any countenance to separation of church and state. Richard B. Barlow, *Citizenship and Conscience: A Study in the Theory and Practice of Religious Toleration in England during the Eighteenth Century* (Philadelphia: University of Pennsylvania Press, 1962), pp. 237, 245-7, 264-8.

4. Charles H. O'Brien, 'Ideas of Religious Toleration at the Time of Joseph II: A Study of the Enlightenment among Catholics in Austria,' *Transactions oj the American Philosophical Society* n.s. 59, 7 (1969), 1-80.

5. Maureen Wall, 'Catholic Loyalty to King and Pope in eighteenth-century Ireland,' *Proceedings of the Irish Catholic Historical Committee 1960* (Dublin: M. H. Gill and Son Ltd., 1960), pp. 17-24.

6. O'Connell kept a journal intermittently as a young man *Daniel O'Connell: His Early Life and Journal 1795 to 1802*, ed. Arthur Houston (London: Sir Isaac Pitman and Sons, Ltd., 1960). In it he frequently lists the books he is reading and sometimes expresses his opinions of them. Many statements in the journal and its general tone are proof of his rationalism.

7. In 1803 he was still a rationalist since he wrote to his wife who was ill: 'If I were a religionist I should spend every moment in praying for you: and this miserable philosophy which I have taken up and been proud of in the room of religion, affords

me now no consolation in my misery (O'Connell to Mary O'Connell, 1 Feb. 1803, *The Correspondence of Daniel O'Connell*, ed. Maurice R. O'Connell [New York: Barnes and Noble, 1973] I, Letter 85). By 1809 he had recovered his religious belief and was a practising Catholic since his wife informed him: 'I can't tell you what real happiness it gives me to have you this sometime back say your prayers and attend Mass so regularly, not to say anything of your observance of the days of abstinence' (Mary O'Connell to O'Connell, 21 Mar. 1809, Ibid., I, Letter 237).

8. This evidence is found in O'Connell's correspondence with one of his uncles (O'Connell to Maurice O'Connell, 3 and 23 Jan. 1797, O'Connell, *Correspondence of O'Connell*, I, Letters 24a and 25: Maurice O'Connell to O'Connell, 30 Jan. 1800, MS 15473, National Library of Ireland).

9. Watson's *Dublin Almanack* for 1800 lists 160 men as called to the Irish Bar during the five-year period 1795-1799. A perusal of the names suggests that fully 100 were definitely Protestants and possibly a majority of the remaining 60. In 1844 Charles Gavan Duffy thought the proportion of Catholics at the Irish Bar to be currently less than a quarter (*Nation*, 2 Mar. 1844). This was an impressionistic estimate but it does indicate that the number of Catholic law students and young barristers about the year 1800 must have been very small.

10. O'Connell repeatedly mentions Bennett in his journal. Their friendship was to last a lifetime.

11. Houston, p. 197.

12. This is known from letters to his wife in November and December 1804 (O'Connell, *Correspondence of O'Connell*, I, Letters 123, 125, 131, 133, 134 and 136).

13. *The Correspondent* (a Dublin newspaper), 5 March 1807.

14. *Dublin Evening Post*, 30 December 1813. The speech is published in *Life and Speeches of Daniel O'Connell*, ed. John O'Connell (Dublin: James Duffy, 1846), II, p. 264

15. John O'Connell, II, p. 264. This book gives 24 October 1817 as the date of the speech but internal evidence proves that the year was 1818. The exact date may have been 24 August since O'Connell was in Tralee at the assizes at that time.

16. O'Connell to Goldsmid, 11 September 1829, O'Connell, *Correspondence of O'Connell*, IV, Letter 1604.

17. O'Connell, *Correspondence of O'Connell*, IV, Letter 1709.

18. *The Times*, 10 March 1831.

19. 17 April 1837, *Mirror of Parliament*, 1837, II, p. 1063.

20. 10 March 1837, Ibid., p. 594. O'Connell's assessment of opinion in Rome was unduly optimistic.

21. Jules Gondon, *Biographie de Daniel O'Connell* (Paris: Sagnier et Bray, 1847).

22. This privilege enabled its holder to have Mass celebrated in his private apartment when away from home.

23. Gondon, pp. 96-97.

24. Ibid., p. 97. The grant was made on 23 September 1838. On 17 March 1838, Gregory granted two indulgences to O'Connell and his family, and on 15 July 1838 one to any persons who prayed in his family oratory at Derrynane. The rescripts for all these privileges were presented by me to the Commissioners of Public Works for exhibition at Derrynane, now a national monument. O'Connell must have kept these privileges from public notice since no writer except Gondon mentioned any of them until the rescripts were made available to J. J. O'Kelly (Sceilg) who cited them in the appendix in his book, *O'Connell Calling: the Liberator's Place in the World* (Tralee: the Kerryman, 1950).

25. O'Connell to Wiseman, 7 November 1836 (St John's Seminary, Wonersh, Guildford, Surrey).

26. O'Connell to William Howitt, 7 November 1836 (Boston Public Library, MS Eng. 144, Whitney fund, 031). Howitt did not become editor though he appears to have remained on friendly relations with O'Connell since he stayed as his guest at Derrynane some years later.

27. *The Speeches and Public Letters of the Liberator*, ed. Mary F. Cusack (Dublin: McGlashan & Gill, 1875), II, pp. 285-6.

28. *O'Connell Centenary Record 1875* (Dublin: Joseph Dollard, 1878), p. 500.

29. Gioacchino Ventura da Raulica, *Elogio funebre di Daniello O'Connnell* . . . (Roma: coi tipi di Giovanni B. Zampi, 1847), p. 105.

30. Henri Dominique Lacordaire, *Eloge Funèbre de Daniel O'Connell* . . . (Paris: Dagnier et Bray, 1848). pp. 28-9.

31. Debate of 26 April 1883, *Hansard*, 3rd Series, CCLXXVIII, pp. 1190-91. O'Connell's statement is ineptly phrased but Gladstone quoted it correctly as reported in the *Mirror of Parliament*, 1834. I, p. 214. A few moments before making this statement O'Connell said: 'I think there ought to be no punishment for libels against Christianity.'

32. The last four paragraphs of this article as published in *Thought* are omitted from the present publication because I see them as irrelevant. They deal with O'Connell's attitude to the Irish Colleges Bill of 1845. The article however, is concerned with religious freedom in relation to the state, not with how a church organizes the education of its congregation.

Chapter Three: *The eighteenth-century background*

1 *The Correspondence of Daniel O'Connell* (Dublin, 1972-1980).

2. On the particular point of O'Connell's attitude to the Gaelic language, see Chapter 4 (pp. 58-59).

3. Some interesting comments on the political attitudes of Gaelic Ireland have been made by the late Rev. Francis Shaw, S.J., Professor of Early and Medieval Irish, University College, Dublin, in his article 'The Canon of Irish History — A Challenge,' *Studies*, LXI, no. 242 (Summer 1972), 113-53,

4. The celebrated seventeenth-century Gaelic history of Ireland known as the *Annals of the Four Masters* recognized Charles I in its preamble as King of Ireland.

5. Maureen Wall, 'Catholic Loyalty to King and Pope in Eighteenth-Century Ireland,' *Proceedings of the Irish Catholic Historical Committee, 1960* (Dublin, 1961), pp. 17-24.

6. Mrs M. J, O'Connell, *The Last Colonel of the Irish Brigade* (London: Kegan Paul, Trench, Trübner & Co., 1892), I, 207-8.

7. O'Connell, *Correspondence of O'Connell*, I, Letters 24a and 25.

8. Since O'Connell was a rationalist at this time it seems more appropriate to describe him as a 'member of the Catholic community' than as a Catholic. He never broke openly with the Church (until his journal was published in 1906 historians did not know that he had ever lost his religious belief); and his attendance and speech at the Catholic meeting in Dublin in 1800 indicate that he was publicly identifying himself as a Catholic.

9. This report is taken from the *Dublin Evening Post* of 14 January 1800.

10. Hunting-Cap to O'Connell, 30 Jan. 1800 (N.L.I., MS 15473).

11. Hunting-Cap did not come forward as an early advocate of the Union. On 28 June 1799, Robert Day, a Justice of the King's Bench in Ireland, wrote to the Earl of Glandore, a North Kerry landlord and the Governor of the county. His epistle included the advice: 'Do not fail to address a flattering letter to Maurice O'Connell, the King of the Romans, who is one of the few of any respectability in our county who have not to my knowledge declared in favour of the measure' (N.L.I., Talbot-Crosbie Papers). The advice must have been taken, since Glandore later informed Castlereagh, the Chief Secretary in Dublin Castle, that Hunting-Cap's name had been added to the Kerry declaration in favour of the Union. He described Hunting-Cap as 'a very sensible man, of considerable property both landed and personal and of great influence amongst the Roman Catholics, by whom he is considered as the head of the independent part of their communion — I mean such as do not derive immediately under my lord Kenmare.' He added that Hunting-Cap attributed his conversion to Unionism to his (Glandore's) arguments (Glandore to Castlereagh, 16 Aug. 1799, Talbot-Crosbie Papers). For bringing my attention to these letters in the Talbot-Crosbie Papers I am indebted to Dr Anthony P. W. Malcomson.

    Hunting-Cap was to return to the subject of how easily his nephew was influenced by undesirable persons even when a mature man, though, on this latter occasion, it was in reference to business affairs: 'I can scarcely express to you the uneasiness I feel since this matter has occurred to me, well knowing as I before mentioned the softness and facility of your disposition and with what ease designing men may draw you into their measures' (Hunting-Cap to O'Connell, 16 May 1811, O'Connell *Correspondence of O'Connell*, I, Letter 337).

12. O'Connell, *Last Colonel*, I, 264.

13. Ibid., I, 265-66.

14. G. C. Bolton, *The Passing of the Irish Act of Union* (Oxford: Oxford University Press, 1966), pp. 77-81.

15. According to Watson's *Dublin Almanack* for 1800 some 160 men were called to the Irish Bar during the five-year period 1795-1799. A large majority of the names are English-sounding while many of those with distinctively Irish names can be taken as Protestant. Only 3 besides O'Connell had the Gaelic prefix 'O' whereas there are 20 with that preflx listed in the almanack for 1840 as being called to the Bar in the five-year period 1835-1839 (one would have to allow for the fact that some men restored that prefix in the early nineteenth century under the influence of Romanticism, but the comparison is still impressive). In an article, 'The Catholic Bar,' in *The Nation* of 2 March 1844, Charles Gavan Duffy says that less than one-fourth of the Irish Bar are Catholics. That is only an impressionistic estimate but it does indicate that the number of Catholics becoming barristers forty years earlier must have been slight. O'Connell's closest friend in the legal profession in those years was Richard Newton Bennett, a Protestant from Co. Wexford. Bennett is repeatedly mentioned in O'Connell's journal, and their friendship was to endure for a generation.

16. O'Connell, *Select Speeches of O'Connell*, I, 24. When the chairman of the meeting observed that the reference to 'an Irish King' could give rise to 'calumny and misrepresentation' O'Connell assured the audience that he was referring to George III, who was 'abounding in every great and good qualification calculated to make his people happy' (ibid.).

17. Ibid., II, 72.

18. *Dublin Evening Post*, 18 Feb. 1815.

19. In 1847 William Fagan published a long excerpt from this address in his *The Life*

and Times of Daniel O'Connell (Cork: J. O'Brien, 1847), I, 524-26. Fagan's accompanying remarks and the excerpt itself show that the address belongs to the period September 1815-July 1817, but it does not appear to have been published. It was so venemous that Grattan's friends may well have dissuaded him from publishing it, or possibly even delivering it. The omission of any mention of it in contemporary newspapers could raise a doubt as to the veracity of Fagan's excerpt but that doubt cannot be sustained. Grattan's sons, James and Henry, Jr., were adults at the time of the Veto controversy, and Henry, Jr., had written his father's *Memoirs* before the appearance of Fagan's biography of O'Connell. They would surely have protested against the publication of a report so damaging to the popularity of their father's reputation if that report were untrue. Lecky and the editor of O'Connell's correspondence in 1888, William J. FitzPatrick, treated the excerpt as genuine (W. E. H. Lecky, *Leaders of Public Opinion in Ireland* [London: Longmans, Green, and Co., 1903], II, 24; W. J. FitzPatrick, *Correspondence of Daniel O'Connell* [London: John Murray, 1888] I, 60, note 3).
20. Henry Grattan, Jr., *Memoirs of the Life and Times of the Rt. Hon. Henry Grattan* (London: H. Colburn, 1839 et seq.). The first four volumes were reviewed in this article in the *Dublin Review* of September 1843 (vol. 15, no. 29, pp. 20-52). The reviewer was the extremist Irish barrister, Edward V.H. Kennedy (see *DNB*).
21. Wiseman to O'Connell, 15 Dec. 1843, *Irish Monthly*, 11 (1883), 340-41.
22. Alf MacLochlainn, 'Thomas Davis and Irish Racialism,' *Irish Times*, 20 Nov. 1973; Maurice R. O'Connell, 'Thomas Davis: A Destructive Conciliator,' *Irish Times*, 6 Aug. 1974. Davis's ambiguity on the origin and composition of the Irish nation may well have arisen from the fact that he was descended not only from the Cromwellian Protestant family of Atkins but also from the ancient and much more interesting Gaelic Catholic family of O'Sullivan-Bere.
23. A perusal of any edition of Burke's *Landed Gentry of Ireland* indicates that the Protestant Ascendancy had a larger share of Gaelic and Norman-Irish blood than is allowed them by popular opinion or even by historians.

Chapter Four: *Collapse and recovery*

1. Séamas Fenton, 'The Great O'Connell', Part Two, *The Kerryman*, 6 July 1946. President O'Kelly is discreetly described as 'a spectator on a high pedestal'.
2. The Committee did not raise sufficient funds for its purpose but it did succeed in keeping Derrynane in existence until 1964 when the State took responsibility for its preservation, primarily on account of its value as a tourist attraction.
3. Edited by R. Dudley Edwards and T. Desmond Williams. *The Great Famine* is less well written but much sounder in scholarship than the more widely read *The Great Hunger* (1962) by Cecil Woodham-Smith.
4. *The Correspondence of Daniel O'Connell, op. cit.*
5. See Chapter 1 above.
6. *Correspondence of O'Connell, op. cit.*, I, xxix.
7. I am indebted to Dr Kevin Danaher of the Department of Irish Folklore, University College Dublin, for much valuable information on O'Connell as a folk-hero.
8. Thomas Davis Lecture, 'O'Connell in Irish Popular Tradition', delivered on Radio Telefís Éireann, 13 April 1975.
9. 'The Artisans of Dublin and Daniel O'Connell 1830-47: an unquiet liaison', *Irish Historical Studies*, XVII, No. 66 (Sept. 1970), pp. 221-43.

10. Thomas Davis Lecture, 'O'Connell and Social and Economic Change', read on Radio Telefís Éireann, 23 March 1975.
11. Thomas Davis Lecture, 'Daniel O'Connell and the Gaelic Tradition', read on Radio Telefís Éireann, 9 March 1975.
12. 'Revolution and Counter-Revolution' in Michael Tierney, ed., *Daniel O'Connell Nine Centenary Essays* (Dublin, 1949), pp. 151-70. Roche has the best literary style of present-day historians of modern Ireland.
13. See Chapter 2 above. I also published an article along these lines in the *Irish Times* of 4 and 8 March 1971.

Chapter Five: *O'Connell, Young Ireland and violence*

1. Denis Gwynn, *Young Ireland and 1848* (London, 1948), pp. 72-73; Kevin B. Nowlan, *The Politics of Repeal: A Study in the Relations between Great Britain and Ireland, 1841-1850* (London, 1965), pp. 108-10; James C. Beckett, *The Making of Modern Ireland, 1603-1923* (London, 1966), p. 334; Lawrence J. McCaffrey, *The Irish Question, 1800-1922* (Louisville, Ky., 1968), pp. 62-63; Robert Kee, *The Green Flag: A History of Irish Nationalism* (London, 1972), pp. 252-55; Gearóid Ó Tuathaigh, *Ireland Before the Famine, 1798-1848* (Dublin, 1972), p. 195; and R. Dudley Edwards *A New History of Ireland* (Dublin, 1972), p. 170. P. S. O'Hegarty is to some extent an exception. In his *A History of Ireland under the Union* (London, 1952), pp. 265-67, he holds that O'Connell since his imprisonment in 1844 was morbidly concerned for the safety and legality of the Repeal Association, and his introduction of the Peace Resolutions was sincerely meant to serve that purpose. In the recent *Daniel O'Connell and His World* (London, 1975), pp. 80-81, R. Dudley Edwards modifies his interpretation to the extent of leaving uncertain O'Connell's motivation for introducing the Resolutions.
2. *Daniel O'Connell: His Early Life and Journal, 1795-1802*, ed. Arthur Houston (London, 1906), p. 155.
3. Ibid., p. 236.
4. *The Correspondence of Daniel O'Connell*, ed. Maurice R. O'Connell, *op. cit.*, I, Letter 97.
5. Ibid., Letter 858.
6. *Life and Speeches of Daniel O'Connell*, ed. John O'Connell (Dublin, 1846), II, pp. 122- 23.
7. *Correspondence of Daniel O'Connell*, II, Letter 544.
8. *The Times*, 3 Nov. 1829.
9. *Dublin Evening Post*, 3 Nov. 1829.
10. In a letter to the Chief Secretary for Ireland in 1833 O'Connell stated that three of the first four alleged conspirators tried were guilty. He was not divulging a professional confidence in making this statement since he did not defend those four. This letter (*Correspondence of Daniel O'Connell* [Dublin 1976], V, Letter 2016) together with his public statement (see above, note 9) convey the impression that he believed most of the defendants guilty.
11. In this letter (see above note 10) O'Connell praised one of the two judges, Richard Pennefather, for his 'intelligent and judicious humanity' in conducting the trial of the first four defendants.
12. See Chapter 2 above, p. 36.

13. *Dublin Evening Post*, 16 April 1840.
14. Ibid., 23 April 1840.
15. Ibid., 3 October 1840.
16. *The Nation*, 18 November 1843.
17. Ibid., 21 September 1844.
18. Ibid., 10 January 1846.
19. Smith O'Brien to O'Connell, 18 December 1845 (O'Connell Papers 13649, N.L.I.).
20. O'Connell to Smith O'Brien, 20-22 December 1845 (Smith O'Brien Papers, N.L.I., MS 435)..
21. *The Nation*, 21 February 1846.
22. Ibid., 21 March 1846.
23. Ibid., 11 April 1846.
24. Ibid.
25. Ibid., 2 May 1846.
26. Doheny to the *Limerick and Clare Examiner*, 11 May 1846. reprinted in *The Nation*, 16 May 1846.
27. *The Nation*, 9 May 1846.
28. Ibid.
29. Ibid., 16 May 1846.
30. Ibid., 9 May 1846.
31. Ibid., 23 May 1846. Several allusions in Doheny's speech make it clear that he was addressing Irish immigrant workers.
32. Ibid., 30 May 1846.
33. Ibid.
34. Ibid.
35. Ibid.
36. *The Tablet*, 23 May 1846.
37. Ibid., 6 June 1846.
38. *The Nation*, 30 May 1846.
39. *The Times*, 8 June 1846.
40. *Dublin Evening Mail*, 10 June 1846.
41. It is significant that O'Connell never denied having made this statement.
42. *The Nation*, 13 June 1846.
43. Ibid., 20 June 1846.
44. O'Connell to the Repeal Association, 18 June 1846 (*The Nation*, 27 June 1846).
45. *The Nation*, 27 June 1846.
46. Ibid., 11 July 1846.
47. Because of the very convenient timing of the introduction of the eleven bills it might be thought that O'Connell was merely conjuring them up and was not concerned about their enactment. This interpretation of his conduct can be refuted. The split in the Tory party meant that the Whigs could now consider much more radical measures for Ireland than at any former time. Whether or not they intended to pass such measures was another matter. Much would depend on what pressure O'Connell could exert. The most important of the bills comprised a radical land reform. The report of the Devon Commission in the spring of 1845 had brought land reform into practical politics for the first time in O'Connell's public life. Two mild bills had been introduced to Parliament with the Tory Government's approval since then but had not been proceeded with. In his resignation speech at the end of June 1846 Peel stated that if the incoming Whig administration were to bring in a conservative measure of land reform he would support it.

48. The first Catholic Relief Act was passed in 1778, and the Volunteers, then in the process of formation, had nothing to do with it. They did give support to the much less important Act of 1782 but its passing owed as much to the Government and to Grattan as to the Volunteers. See Maurice R. O'Connell, *Irish Politics and Social Conflict in the Age of the American Revolution* (Philadelphia, 1965), chaps. 5 and 13.
49. *The Nation*, 18 October 1845.
50. Ibid., 28 February 1846.
51. Ibid.
52. Ibid., 4 April 1846.
53. Ibid., 23 May 1846.
54. T. M. Ray described Archdeacon as Sub-Secretary in his letter to O'Connell of 13 May 1846 (O'Connell Papers 13646, N.L.I.).
55. *The Nation*, 6 June 1846.
56. Ibid., 4 July 1846.
57. In writing to O'Connell, just after Smith O'Brien had finished his speech, the Secretary of the Repeal Association, T.M. Ray, made the surprising statement: 'He [Smith O'Brien] has just closed his speech, avoiding anything irritating and on the whole excellent in spirit' (Ray to O'Connell, 29 June 1846, O'Connell Papers 13646, N.L.I.). Ray must have been unduly influenced by the goodhumoured and polite tone of the speech. He seems to have ignored the fact that O'Brien devoted the greater part of it to an attack on the renewal of the Whig Alliance, thus indicating there was trouble ahead. There is always the consideration that the report of the speech in the press (the same version appeared in all the newspapers) may have differed from what was actually said, but O'Connell would be concerned with what he, and the public, read. In the absence of a public disclaimer from O'Brien (if his speech had been misreported) O'Connell would be obliged to consider the speech as it appeared in the papers. There was no disclaimer.
58. *The Nation*, 27 June 1846.
59. Ibid., 18 July 1846. The document was printed as presented to the Repeal Association on 13 July
60. The minutes of this meeting, in the handwriting of T. M. Ray is in the Smith O'Brien Papers, MS 437, N.L.I.
61. *The Nation*, 18 July 1846.
62. O'Connell to Edmond Smithwick, 23 June 1846, Papers of Mrs Anne Smithwick, Birchgrove, Kilkenny.
63. O'Connell to Smith O'Brien, 18 July 1846, Smith O'Brien Papers, MS 437, N.L.I.
64. *The Times*, 21 July 1846.

Chapter Six: *O'Connell and his family*
1. Basil O'Connell, 'Catherine O'Mullane', *Irish Genealogist*, II, no. 10 (July 1953), p. 311.
2. Maurice R. O'Connell, ed., *The Correspondence of Daniel O'Connell, op. cit.*, III, Letter 1268, Mary O'Connell to O'Connell, 4 December 1825.
3. *Ibid.*, II, Letter 515, Rickard O'Connell to O'Connell, 4 February 1815.
4. *Ibid.*, I, Letter 72, O'Connell to Mary O'Connell, probably early September 1802.
5. *Ibid.*, I, Letter 148, Jeremiah McCartie to O'Connell, 26 June 1805.
6. *Ibid.*, I, xix.
7. 'O'Connell in Irish Popular Tradition,' Thomas Davis lecture delivered on Radio

Telefís Éireann, 13 April 1975.
8. As a very small child Maurice O'Connell spoke Irish at Carhen (O'Connell, *Correspondence*, op. cit., I, Letters 144 and 146). In his autobiography the famous war correspondent of the Crimea, William Howard Russell, says of his visit to Derrynane in 1845: 'And there was Maurice O'Connell . . . talking Irish with boys and colleens. who laughed at his jokes as if they were at a fair or a wedding' (John B. Atkins, *The Life of Sir William Howard Russell*, London, 1911, I, 33).
9. Maurice R. O'Connell, 'O'Connell Reconsidered,' *Studies*, LXIV, no. 254 (Summer 1975), pp 110-112. In addition to the factors dealt with in this article there is the speech made by Maurice O'Connell in the Repeal Association on 14 June 1847, just a month after his father's death. In this speech Maurice attacked the Young Irelanders for having opposed his father on the subject of moral versus physical force; and he called on Repealers only to support those candidates in the forthcoming general election who believed in moral force (*The Nation*, 19 June 1847).
10. *O'Connell Correspondence*, op. cit., II, Letter 837 O'Connell to Bolivar, 17 April 1820.
11. Ibid., II, Letter 851, Morgan O'Connell to O'Connell, 25 August 1820.
12. Ibid., II, Letter 930, O'Connell to Hunting-Cap, 5 January 1822.
13 Ibid., II, Letter 1011, Mary O'Connell to O'Connell, 20 April 1823.
14. Ibid., II, Letter 1014, O'Connell to Mary O'Connell, 1 May 1823.
15. Ibid., II, Letter 957, O'Connell to Mary O'Connell, 15 April 1822.
16. Ibid., II, Letter 978. Count O'Connell to O'Connell, 5 August 1822.
17. Ibid., II, Letter 1355, Morgan O'Connell to O'Connell, 1 January 1827.
18. *Dublin Evening Post*, 29 May 1858.
19. Ibid.
20. *Freeman's Journal*, 29 May 1858.
21. Alfred Webb, *A Compendium of Irish Biography* (Dublin, 1878), p. 382.
22. The Repeal Association debates were examined as reported in the O'Connellite *Pilot*. This newspaper gave these debates the fullest coverage. I am indebted to Miss May O'Mahony for making this examination.
23. William J. FitzPatrick, ed., *The Correspondence of Daniel O'Connell* (London, 1888), II. pp. 187-92.

Chapter Seven: *Lawyer and landlord*

1. All letters quoted or referred to in this article arc published in Maurice R. O'Connell (ed.), *The Correspondence of Daniel O'Connell* (Dublin, 1972-1980). Since they can easily be identified in the published volumes they are not footnoted in this article.
2. Peel to Viscount Whitworth (successor as Lord-Lieutenant to Richmond), 1 August 1813, Charles S. Parker, (ed.), *Sir Robert Peel* (London, 1891), I, p. 104.
3. Peel to the Earl of Desart, 10 August 1813, Parker, *Peel*, I, pp. 116-117.
4. Sean O'Faoláin, *The King of the Beggars* (London, 1938), p. 204.
5. William Fagan, *The Life and Times of Daniel O'Connell* (Cork, 1847), I, p. 162.
6. *Mirror of Parliament*, 1834, pp. 2849-2850. This report has O'Connell using the word 'Whitefeet' instead of 'Whiteboys', but he must have used, and he certainly meant to use, the latter term. The description 'Whitefeet' was not used before 1830, by which time O'Connell had retired from the Bar. Furthermore, *Hansard* (3rd Series, XXV, p. 296), in a shorter version of his speech, uses the term 'Whiteboyism',

not 'Whitefeet', in its report. O'Connell made a speech of this kind after the conclusion of the Doneraile Conspiracy trials.

7. William Henry Curran, 'Sketches of the Irish Bar — Mr O'Connell', *New Monthly Magazine*, Vol. 8 (1823).
8. Daniel Owen Madden, *Ireland and its Rulers since 1829* (London, 1844), I, pp. 22-5.
9. For a more detailed account of O'Connell's financial position see Chapter 1 above.
10. 'An gheadach d'a crudhadh'san Ghleann', in Seamus Fenton, *Amhráin Thómais Ruaidh, i., The Songs of Tomas Ruadh O'Sullivan, the Iveragh Poet, 1785-1848,* (Dublin, 1914, second edition, 1922), No. XXVII. I am indebted to Dr Padráig de Brún for bringing this poem to my attention.
11. *Evidence taken before Her Majesty's Commissioners of Enquiry into the State of the Law and Practice in respect to the Occupation of Land in Ireland* (Dublin, 1845), Part III, p. 936. O'Connell gave his evidence on 28 January 1845.
12. I am indebted to the late Eugene Ring of Main St., Cahirciveen for the local tradition on Primrose as a land agent.
13. *Beatha Domnaill Uí Chonaill* (Baile Atha Cliath, 1936), p. 198.
14. Foster's strictures on O'Connell appeared in *The Times* of 18 November, 3 and 25 December, and 6 January
15. O'Connell defended himself in speeches in the Repeal Association on 24 November, 1, 8, 15 and 29 December, and 5 January
16. Russell's report appeared in *The Times* of 25 December 1845.
17. John B. Atkins, *The Life of Sir William Howard Russell* (London, 1911), I, pp. 33-34.
18. I am indebted to Sister M. de Lourdes of the Presentation Convent in Cahirciveen, for much information on O'Connell's relations with Cahirciveen.
19. T. Wemyss Reid, *Life of the Rt. Hon. W. E. Forster* (London, 1888), I, pp. 178-81.

Chapter Eight: *Irish constitutionalism: a tradition?*

1. In his *Confrontations: Studies in Irish History* (Totowa, N.J. 1972), pp. 142-51.
2. Reproduced as Chapter 5 above.
3. *A Life Spent for Ireland: Selections from the Journals of W.J. O'Neill Daunt edited by his Daughter* (Irish University Press, 1972), pp. 56-57.
4. The correspondence between Dr Harriman and myself is in the National Library of Ireland, MS 28, 895.
5. *The Correspondence of Daniel O'Connell, op. cit.*, VIII.
6. Charles Gavan Duffy, *Four Years of Irish History 1845-1849* (London, 1883), p. 270; *My Life in Two Hemispheres* (London, 1898), I, p. 174n.
7. *Correspondence of O'Connell, op. cit.*, VIII.
8. Denny Lane to Thomas Davis, 16 June 1845 Davis Papers, N.L.I., MS 2644, ff. 145-60.
9. Repeal Association, 14 and 21 June 1847 (*Dublin Evening Post*, 15 and 22 June, 1847).
10. *The Nation*, 12 June 1847.
11. Sean MacBride, *A Message to the Irish People* (Mercier Press, Dublin and Cork, 1985), p. 31.
12. *Catholic Historical Review*, LXXIV, no. 2 (April 1988), pp. 119-225.
13. This interference with the rights of property would be contrary to the English constitutional tradition, at least since the time of the Declaration of Rights of 1689. For

the interpretation of Section 3 I am indebted to Gerard A. Lee. S.C. of the Irish Bar.
14. *Limerick Reporter and Tipperary Vindicator*, 25 Feb. 1851.
15. Ibid., 7 March 1851.
16. John O'Connell to the Mayor of Limerick, 3 March 1851; Ibid., 7 March 1851.
17. Ibid., 7 March 1851.
18. London, 1886, 139-40.
19. *Dublin Evening Post*, 27 Dec. 1853.

Chapter Nine: *Ireland, Irish-Americans and Negro Slavery*

1. Gilbert Osofsky, 'Abolitionists, Irish Emigrants and the Dilemmas of Romantic
   Nationalism', *American Historical Review*, LXXX, No. 4 (Oct. 1975), pp. 889-912
   (Osofsky died before completing his article which probably explains why he says
   little of Romantic Nationalism); Douglas Riach, 'Daniel O'Connell and American
   anti-slavery', *Irish Historical Studies*, XX, No. 77 (March 1976), pp. 3-25; Neil J.
   O'Connell, O.F.M., 'Irish Emancipation — Black Abolition: A Broken Partnership',
   Robert Noltman, ed., *The Consortium on Revoluntionary Europe Proceedings 1978*
   (Athens, Ga., 1980), pp. 58-76; Owen Dudley Edwards, 'The American Image of
   Ireland: A Study of its Early Phases', *Perspectives in American History, Vol. IV 1970*
   (Harvard University, 1970, no editor named), pp. 199-282.
2. *The Nation*, 13 Jan. 1844.
3. *The Nation*, 5 Apr. 1845.
4. *The Nation*, 12 Apr. 1845.
5. *The Nation*, 9 Aug. 1845.
6. *The Nation*, 9 Aug. 1845. Davis's correspondence shows that he was presently acting
   as editor of *The Nation* in the absence of its owner-editor, Charles Gavan Duffy, a
   fact attested to by Duffy himself in his *Young Ireland* (New York, 1881), pp. 730 et
   seq. Furthermore, there is something of Davis's style in the editorial.
7. *The Nation*, 16 Jan. 1847.
8. *The Nation*, 13 Feb. 1847.
9. *The Nation*, 20 Feb. 1847.
10. *The Nation*, 10 Apr. 1847
11. *The Nation*, 1 May, 1847.
12. Samuel Haughton, *Memoir of James Haughton* (Dublin 1877), p. 80.
13. The letter was taken from the *Daily Enquirer* of Cincinnati and was published in the
    Dublin *Pilot* of 12 April 1844.
14. Carter G. Woodson, 'The Negroes of Cincinnati prior to the Civil War', *Journal of
    Negro History*, Vol. I, No. 1 (January 1916), pp. 5, 8-9, 12-13.
15 Leonard L. Richards, *'Gentlemen of Property and Standing' : Anti-Abolition Mobs
    in Jacksonian America* (Oxford University Press, 1971), pp. 34-35, 40-43, 92-100,
    113, 122-29.
16. The address was adopted by the Repeal Association at their meeting on 11 October,
    and was transcribed in the report of that meeting in *The Nation* of 14 October 1843.
17. Owen Dudley Edwards, *op. cit.*, p. 270.
18. Joseph Lee, 'The Social and Economic Ideas of O'Connell', Kevin B. Nowlan and
    Maurice R. O'Connell, eds., *Daniel O'Connell: Portrait of a Radical* (Belfast 1984),
    p. 82.

Bibliography

of all useful and/or authoritative modern books on O'Connell

McCartney, Donal, ed. *The World of Daniel O'Connell.* Dublin: Mercier Press, 1980. Fourteen articles, mostly of high quality, describing O'Connell's image abroad, his role in the British Parliament, his attitude to Black slavery, and his influence on the Liberal Catholic movement in Western Europe.

MacDonagh, Oliver. *The Hereditary Bondsman: Daniel O'Connell 1775-1829.* London: Weidenfeld and Nicolson, 1988. *The Emacipationist: Daniel O'Connell 1830-1847.* London: Weidenfield and Nicholson, 1989. These two books may well be judged the outstanding biography of O'Connell.

Macintyre, Angus. *The Liberator: Daniel O'Connell and the Irish Party 1830-1847.* London: Hamish Hamilton, 1965. A detailed and very useful account of O'Connell's role in the Whig Government's Irish legislation 1831-1840.

Moley, Raymond. *Daniel O'Connell: Nationalism Without Violence.* New York: Fordham University Press, 1974. A popular biography by a distinguished American political commentator.

Nowlan, Kevin B., and Maurice O'Connell, eds. *Daniel O'Connell: Portrait of a Radical.* New York: Fordham University Press, 1985. Eight articles on various aspects of O'Connell, notably his association with Gaelic Ireland, his social and economic ideas, and his role in British politics.

O'Connell, Daniel. *The Correspondence of Daniel O'Connell.* Edited by Maurice R. O'Connell. Dublin: Irish University Press, Government Stationery Office, Blackwater Press, 1972-1980. Thirty-five hundred private letters to and from O'Connell.

O'Faoláin, Sean. *King of the Beggars: A Life of Daniel O'Connell, the Irish Liberator in a Study of the Rise of the Modern Irish Democracy.* London: Nelson, 1938. Entertaining biographical study of O'Connell's Personality. Intuitive rather than scholarly, it is one of the very few works on O'Connell before 1965 that merits consideration.

O'Ferrall, Fergus. *Catholic Emancipation Daniel O'Connell and the Rise of Irish Democracy 1820-30*. Atlantic Highlands, N.J.: Humanities Press International, 1985. Comprehensive study of the Catholic Association as the modern world's first democratic mass movement. Both grass-roots organization and its effect on high politics are described.
O'Ferrall, Fergus. *Daniel O'Connell*. Dublin: Gill and Macmillan, 1981. Short but academically able biography.
Trench, Charles Chenevix. *The Great Dan: A Biography of Daniel O'Connell*. London: Jonathan Cape, 1984. Historically sound and entertaining, this biography is written with wit and insight.

Index